Reader's Digest
Wildlife Watch

Waterside & Coast in Winter

Reader's Digest
Wildlife Watch

Waterside & Coast in Winter

Published by
The Reader's Digest Association Limited
London • New York • Sydney • Montreal

Wildlife habitats and havens

Coast watch

Animals and plants in focus

Waterside watch

Introduction

Gripped by the bitter chill of winter, the withered, pale brown foliage and feathery seedheads of a vast East Anglian reedbed remain motionless. The stems, stiffened by frost, are locked together and shackled in a prison of ice. There is no rustling of the reeds in the breeze, for the freezing air has struck them dumb, and for much of the time no sound at all emanates from the beds.

Then, at the foot of the reeds, there is a barely detectable flicker of movement as a dark bird with a long red bill slips out from between the stems into the open. It is a water rail, a relative of the moorhen, and a bird so secretive that it is rarely seen. The harsh conditions have flushed it out in search of food, its normally sleek plumage fluffed up against the cold. Usually it feeds on fish, frogs and other small animals, but in midwinter it will eat almost anything, even attacking smaller birds roosting among the reeds. Its survival in such conditions seems almost miraculous, yet there it is – proof that even in the dead of winter, there is life.

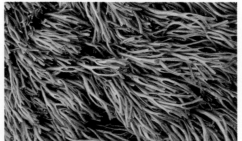

◀ In icy weather the flash of the kingfisher's brilliant plumage can be seen on rivers and streams, and also on estuaries, where it hunts alongside winter waders.

▲ Cold weather has little effect on seaweeds of tidal shores such as this channelled wrack, but seasonal storms may rip some species away from the rocks and dump them high on the shore.

▲ Southern and western coasts often attract wintering black redstarts, which can be seen running over rocky shores or combing the strand line in search of invertebrates. This is a male – the female is drabber.

Icy waters

The water rail is not the only elusive water bird making its presence known on this raw winter morning. At intervals a curious low coughing grunt drifts across the marsh. This is the call of a bittern – quite different from the male's booming 'song', which is heard in spring. Bitterns (see pages 54–59) are among the rarest breeding birds in Britain, but in winter their numbers are swelled somewhat by migrants from the Continent, where the winters are much harsher. Even so, they are still extremely difficult to see, and the distinctive calls are usually the only clue to their presence.

By contrast, the bittern's close relative, the grey heron, is a constant but wary presence by the water. On the frozen marsh it often has trouble finding food, although – frustratingly – it may be able to see fish, and even frogs, active beneath the ice. It fares better on the margins of rivers, where the flowing water is less likely to freeze over. Standing motionless in the shallows, it watches intently for

prey, preferably big, meaty fish, such as eels or the bottom-feeding barbel (see pages 75–78). Spearing or seizing them with its long, sharp bill, it may be able to swallow them whole, but it takes its biggest catches to the bank to eat piecemeal.

The heron competes for prey with an exotic hunter that escaped from fur farms to live on British rivers – the American mink. Often confused with the similar but much larger otter, the mink is bolder, more widespread and more likely to be seen during a winter walk beside a river. Its glossy, chocolate-brown coat looks almost black, especially when wet, and mink often sit by the river, grooming their fur. They are notorious for catching and eating water voles, and are often blamed for that species' decline, but they also eat plenty of fish. To fish farmers who raise rainbow trout – another American introduction (see pages 71–74) – a visit from a mink is like having a fox raid the henhouse.

Flooded meadows

One reason why mink have had such an impact on water voles is that the habitat available to voles is usually restricted to a narrow strip of river bank, and the voles have few places where they can hide. Most of the marshy flood plains that once flanked lowland

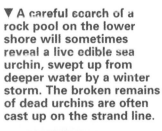

▼ A careful search of a rock pool on the lower shore will sometimes reveal a live edible sea urchin, swept up from deeper water by a winter storm. The broken remains of dead urchins are often cast up on the strand line.

▲ The skulking water rail has a narrow body adapted for slipping noiselessly between reed stems, but it often betrays its presence by giving strange pig-like grunts and squeals from dense cover.

► An opportunist hunter, the American mink takes a wide range of prey from fish to voles, rabbits and water birds, such as moorhens.

rivers, with their creeks, ditches and pools, have now been drained and converted into fertile farmland. Yet some flood plains remain in their semi-wild state, and are even allowed to flood in wet winters (see pages 12–15). They provide vital domains for a wide variety of waterside life, including water voles, and are among the last places in the lowlands where resident waders, such as the long-billed snipe (see pages 67–70), still breed in spring and summer.

In winter these natural flood plains attract flocks of migrant birds, especially waders and wildfowl. The worms, insect grubs and other invertebrates that are flushed out of the soil by floodwater are sought by lapwings. Despite their white and iridescent bronze-green plumage, these birds can be surprisingly hard to see when standing still on the damp grass in dull winter light. Once one is noticed, however, it soon becomes apparent that they are everywhere, dotted over the flood meadow like small, wispy-crested sentinels. The appearance of a hunting peregrine in the sky – indicated by a silhouette like a black anchor, high overhead – will often put lapwings up in a spectacular wheeling flock, their black-and-white wings flashing against the dark clouds.

When these meadows flood, their waters provide food and refuge for a dazzling variety of ducks, such as the wigeon,

teal, pintail and shoveler. Ducks moult into their breeding colours early in the year, and the males are at their most resplendent in winter when the light reflected off the floodwater illuminates every exquisite detail of their plumage. They take the opportunity to pair up before migration, and the clear, whistling '*whee-oo*' calls of male wigeon are among the most evocative sounds of winter wetlands. Unlike most ducks, wigeon feed largely on grass, and they can often be seen working their way over the pasture in dense flocks that resemble mobile carpets of rich, varied colour.

Living mud

If birds are the most eye-catching visitors to freshwater wetlands, they dominate the scene on coasts and estuaries. Favoured sites can attract winter migrants in their thousands, particularly small waders. The knot, for instance, may gather in such vast numbers that airborne flocks look like clouds of smoke billowing off the mudflats and shingle banks. Recognising these coastal waders in their greyish winter plumage can be a challenge (see pages 112–119), especially when they are feeding far from the shore, but even if their identity is uncertain, they still make an unforgettable impression.

▼ Most rock pool animals are active throughout the winter. They include the hermit crab, famous for the way it protects its vulnerable body by adopting the empty shell of a dead mollusc, such as a whelk.

▲ Waterside vegetation dies back in winter, increasing the chance of seeing a water shrew. Like all shrews it is a voracious feeder that has to eat its own weight in food every day, so it spends much of its time hunting.

▲ Boldly patterned plumage and a bright red bill make the shelduck a conspicuous bird of tidal estuaries. It is one of the largest ducks seen in Britain, and the male has a distinctive knob at the base of the bill.

Some of the largest concentrations of winter waders are to be seen on estuaries (see pages 22–27), where the deep, organically rich mud of the intertidal mudflats supports dense concentrations of burrowing worms and grazing molluscs, such as the peppery furrow shell, the cockle and the tiny laver spire shell. As the tide ebbs, the birds leave their roosts at the top of the shore and follow the receding waterline, probing and picking at the wet mud. Not all the mollusc-eating shore-dwelling birds are waders – the laver spire shell is a favourite food of the colourful shelduck, which strains them from the mud by sweeping its broad, flat bill from side to side through the liquefied surface.

The tide-washed sand of sheltered beaches (see pages 28–33) is almost as densely populated with burrowing urchins, molluscs and worms. This is often apparent from the many coiled casts of lugworms that appear on the lower shore at low tide (see pages 122–123). Their significance is not lost on long-billed waders, such as the curlew, which stalks slowly over the gleaming sand watching for the chance to seize a worm as it backs up its burrow to void its cast at the surface.

Rich pickings

When the rising tide floods the beach, hungry fish such as plaice, flounder and bass swim inshore to browse on the extended tentacles and feeding tubes of the worms and shellfish. Off many rocky shores, submerged shore life also attracts sea ducks, such as the eider, common scoter, long-tailed duck and goldeneye (see pages 60–66), which dive below the surface to gather molluscs and crustaceans. On remote northern and western coasts they may be joined by hunting otters, which prey mainly on crabs and fish (see pages 84–87).

Beaches can be bleak, windswept places in winter, but the seasonal storms bring their own rewards for coastal wildlife, dumping dislodged seaweeds, shattered shellfish, drowned seabirds and even the odd dead whale high on the strand line (see pages 34–37). This heap of detritus is a rich source of food for scavenging birds such as crows and herring gulls (see pages 100–105), as well as beachcombing land mammals, such as foxes and rats. For some of these animals, the assorted decaying debris can be a seasonal lifeline, providing vital, if barely palatable, food to see them through the darkest, hardest days of winter.

▲ Glasswort is one of the few flowering plants able to survive long periods submerged by salt water. It colonises the tidal mudflats that fringe coastal salt marshes, and has succulent, easily broken stems.

▼ Many freshwater invertebrates remain active in winter, provided the water does not freeze solid. The ramshorn snail can often be seen using its rasping tongue to graze algae from submerged pond plants and rocks.

▶ Although now in serious decline as a breeding bird in Britain, the lapwing is very numerous in winter when its numbers are boosted by European migrants. It often forms large flocks on flood meadows.

Wildlife habitats and havens

- Flood plain wildlife
- Lowland river walk
- Where rivers meet the sea
- Sandy shore – life underfoot
- Strand line wildlife
- The Lake District – panoramic country

Flood plain wildlife

Swollen rivers have been spilling out over the land for thousands of years, creating broad, fertile flood plains. In winter, such flooding transforms the countryside into a magnet for wetland wildlife.

The weather systems that sweep in from the cold Atlantic in winter bring grey skies and heavy rain to much of Britain. As the water drains off the higher land, many lowland streams and rivers swell to the point where they burst their banks and inundate the surrounding landscape. Such flooding is often seen as a natural disaster, and some floods can indeed cause considerable damage to crops and property. Yet winter flooding is a natural phenomenon, and for wildlife it is often highly beneficial. Far from being destructive, these winter floods may create and regularly revive a wonderfully rich habitat – the flood plain.

Flood plains flank the slow, often meandering middle reaches of rivers flowing towards tidal estuaries. They are the result of centuries of winter flooding by water that is cloudy with fine silt. As the water spreads out across the land it stops flowing, enabling the suspended silt particles to settle on the submerged ground. Over time, the deposits from successive floods build up to create an area of flat land flanking the river, and filling the bottom of the valley. In its natural state, such a flood plain is threaded with drainage channels and dotted with marshy wetlands and tangled willow beds. This varied environment attracts many species of wild plants and animals, which have evolved ways of exploiting the benefits on offer.

Tough plants

The plants that grow on these natural flood plains must be tolerant of silty, waterlogged soils. They have to survive being underwater for long periods in winter, yet be able to spend months with their roots imprisoned in sun-baked clay in summer. They must also be tough enough to grow up through the silt and debris that are dumped by the floodwaters.

◀ **Winter visitors to Britain, white-fronted geese often feed on the grass and clover that grow on flood plains.**

▼ **Flooded pastures flank some lowland rivers in winter, turning the whole area into a series of broad, shallow lakes.**

Many grasses are well equipped to thrive in these conditions, and some are highly palatable to grazing animals, making excellent pasture. They include species such as floating sweet-grass, marsh foxtail, meadow foxtail and reed sweet-grass, all of which will grow in shallow water. Many sedges and rushes also grow in the wet soils of flood meadows. They are less attractive to grazing animals, so overgrazed meadows tend to lose their grasses and become overgrown with sedges and rushes.

Fertile soils

Since the silt deposited by floodwater is rich in organic matter, the soil it creates is very fertile. From the 16th to the 18th centuries, farmers in the south of England made the most of this by deliberately flooding fields to boost their productivity. They dug

◄ The dried-out flower heads of purple loosestrife often persist through the winter on the overgrown, damp margins of drainage ditches and pools.

► Where they are not heavily grazed, wetland grasses such as floating sweet-grass may form dense stands of tall stems that bear feathery seed heads.

channels to carry water from the main river across the fields. These were blocked at the other end, so when the water level rose it trickled over the edges of the channels and flowed gently over the fields. Here it slowly permeated the soil, depositing its load of silt, before draining back to the main river via a network of ditches and sluices.

The best time to flood these watermeadows was in January and February, when the relatively warm water from the chalk streams would keep the winter frosts away from the grass and stimulate its growth. The meadows could then support sheep or cattle a few weeks earlier than unmanaged meadows. When the livestock

were removed, the meadow could be flooded again to stimulate further growth ready for the summer hay crop. In very dry years, the meadow would sometimes be flooded again in the autumn. This alternation of grazing and flooding recreated the natural pattern of winter flooding in flood plains in a controlled way, resulting in highly productive meadows.

Today this labour-intensive practice has almost died out, but with renewed interest in organic farming methods, the technique is being revived in a few places. In most valleys, however, the fertile soils have been drained and turned into arable fields. Also, many rivers are now controlled with weirs and flood banks, making winter floods a thing of the past. In some places, though, areas have been set aside to absorb floodwater caused by heavy rainfall, and these uncultivated areas retain – or

soon regain – the character of natural flood plains, with all their wild, luxuriant beauty.

Winter wildfowl
In East Anglia, for example, drainage could not solve the problem of severe winter flooding in this flat landscape. So the area between the artificial New Bedford River and the original river course

was set aside as a place where floodwater can collect, leaving the fields on either side relatively dry. This managed flood plain, known as the Ouse Washes, is visited by tens of thousands of wildfowl every winter and contains important nature reserves.

Many other nature reserves are also managed in this way, providing vital winter

FLOOD DISPERSAL

Many fish, pond snails, freshwater shrimps and water slaters live in isolated pools. In the normal course of events, they are unlikely to come into contact with other communities and this means that the gene pool is restricted. Floods are often the means by which these creatures find their way into new habitats, enabling them to start new colonies or interbreed with established populations. A major flood will wash large numbers of creatures out of their ponds and disperse them over a wide area, and while many will be swept to their doom, some will reach new places that suit them. This is why newly created ponds or recently cleared ditches are rapidly colonised after winter flooding.

► The lesser whirlpool ramshorn snail is confined to ditches in just a few flood plains in southern England, and relies on flooding to spread to new sites.

◄ Freshwater shrimps are common on wetlands, but their occurrence in any locality is strongly influenced by winter flooding.

The skylark can find plenty of food on a fertile flood plain. In winter, these streaked brown birds may forage on the ground, where they can be hard to see.

Controlled seasonal grazing by cattle or ponies is the most efficient and wildlife-friendly way to manage flood-prone grasslands.

Flood plains require careful management to maintain their diverse nature. The most effective way of doing this is to use grazing animals such as cattle. If there is no grazing, the flora will be succeeded by damp woodland dominated by willows, alder and birch. Overgrazing, on the other hand, favours tough sedges, rushes and other unpalatable species. So careful planning is essential. The traditional strategy is to cut the meadows for hay in summer and then allow livestock in to graze them for a few months before the winter floods return.

Large animals such as cattle also create micro-habitats, by making deep hoofprints in soft mud while leaving some plants such as tussock-forming sedges untouched. Lapwings favour the dried-out hoofprints as nesting sites, while snipe and redshank use the tussocks for shelter. Skylarks make use of closely grazed turf for their neatly woven grass nests, and migrant yellow wagtails hop around the feet of the cattle, snapping up the insects that they disturb as they graze.

sanctuaries for the wildfowl that flock to Britain to escape the harsh winters of their Arctic breeding grounds. They include whooper swans from Iceland and Bewick's swans from Siberia, which congregate on the flooded grasslands to fatten up after the rigours of breeding. They are joined by various species of geese and a huge range of ducks including the tiny teal, elegant pintail, big-billed shoveler and stocky pochard.

This vast array of birds requires a huge winter food supply. There is always plenty for seed and plant-eating waterfowl, such as swans and geese. The roots, tubers and other underground parts of flood-meadow plants are all highly nutritious and usually abundant. Furthermore, since each species is adapted to feed in a different way, there is little competition between them. Dabbling ducks up-end in the shallows to reach their food, while diving ducks can feed in the deepest floods. Long-necked swans stretch down to reach plants growing in deeper water, while geese are more suited to grazing on land, where they use their strong beaks to crop grasses and clovers.

As winter flood waters rise, soil organisms such as beetle grubs and earthworms are flushed out of the earth and taken by dabbling ducks and waders such as snipe and redshank. The seeds of rushes and sedges, which can be found in the mud, are favoured by small dabbling ducks. Meanwhile, the ditches and weed-choked channels that criss-cross the flood plains are patrolled by moorhens, water rails and sometimes the rare, elusive bittern. When they are not feeding, many of these birds roost on rafts of vegetation floating on the water, or on temporary islands where they are safe from ground predators, such as prowling foxes.

Blaze of colour

As winter gives way to spring, many of the wildfowl leave for their northern breeding grounds, while the more dramatic plant life of flood meadows starts to assert itself. Common club-rush – actually a sedge – springs up in the drainage channels, and the green blades of common reed and bulrush sprout from

◄ Floods often freeze over in the dead of winter, forcing waterbirds such as these swans and ducks to jostle for space on any remaining open water.

The short-eared owl may frequent the margins of flood meadows in winter, watching for small mammals that have been displaced by rising waters.

among the dead brown foliage that often all but chokes the pools and ditches. Before long, more colourful plants burst into bloom. Marsh marigold and lesser spearwort often flower in their thousands in spring, while later in the year the river banks, drainage channels and pools glow with yellow flag iris and the tall spires of purple loosestrife. The frothy pink heads of hemp agrimony, sky-blue spikes of water forget-me-not and domed white umbels of hemlock together with water dropwort and wild angelica add even more colour to the scene.

Away from the ditches, the wet grasslands support yet more beautiful species, such as common meadow rue and the heavily scented meadowsweet. Marsh helleborine may flower

in summer, where earlier in the year cuckooflower blossomed and attracted the dainty orange-tip butterfly. Smaller or less conspicuous wet meadow flowers include marsh bedstraw, greater bird's-foot trefoil and the creeping marsh pennywort. In some of the more fertile flood meadows, 60 different species of wild flowers and up to 30 different species of grasses, sedges and rushes may thrive. Many are excellent sources of nectar for hoverflies and other true flies, butterflies and bees. The smaller flies attract predatory dragonflies.

Natural flood plains are well worth exploring at any time of year but in winter, when the floodwaters transform the landscape into a mirror of the sky and the wildfowl flock in their thousands, flood plains become truly special.

As it meanders towards the sea, the River Cuckmere in Sussex lays down the layers of silt that have created its flat flood plain.

▲ A flooded meadow provides rich pickings for a sharp-eyed grey heron, ready to snap up anything from an eel to a vole that has been flooded out of its run.

◄ Amphibians, such as this palmate newt, arrive in flood-plain pools and channels to spawn as early as mid-February.

WILDLIFE WATCH

Where can I see flood plains?

● Many lowland rivers are no longer allowed to flood in winter, although the flood plains are still there. However, good examples of winter flooding can still be seen near Fordingbridge in Hampshire. Here the flood meadows on the River Avon attract large flocks of wildfowl in winter.

● In Somerset, the once extensive Levels still flood when heavy rainfall causes the Rivers Axe and Parrett to burst their banks.

● The River Ouse in Yorkshire floods regularly, but the best examples of flood meadows are to be found on the Ouse Washes in the East Anglian Fenlands. Here the river is allowed to flood each winter. The floods attract thousands of migrant wildfowl, and when the water drains away the grasslands are important summer breeding grounds for waders. Heavy winter rainfall may also cause floods on the nearby River Nene.

Lowland river walk

The peace and quiet of an overgrown riverside track or footpath may be broken by the occasional bird call or the rustling of undergrowth, indicating that a squirrel or fox is on the move, in search of food.

A brisk walk down a river path in winter can be an exhilarating experience. The ground may be muddy and slippery underfoot – if it is not frozen solid – and the wind may be rather too cold for comfort, but the sudden flash of a kingfisher or the glow of bright willow shoots against a clear blue sky soon provides a welcome distraction.

The most rewarding river walks are to be found along the wilder stretches, away from built-up reaches that pass through towns, where straightened banks are reinforced with concrete and steel. The native riverside vegetation is vital for animals, especially in winter when small birds and mammals need to find shelter from the windchill. Natural, soft river banks are essential for burrowing water voles, and marginal reedbeds provide cover for waterfowl. So although an urban stretch of river may spring the odd wildlife surprise, the real interest is to be found where the concrete stops, and the river has been allowed to find its own winding way through the landscape.

Swan flotillas

The most conspicuous birds of the river are waterfowl, and especially the mute swans that live on many lowland rivers in Britain. Badly hit by lead poisoning from the 1960s to 1980s, populations are now increasing thanks to a ban on lead fishing weights. In spring, mute swans occupy traditional breeding territories, but in winter they live in flocks that comprise both snow white adults with orange bills and less immaculate immature birds with grey-brown plumage and grey bills. The flocks roam nomadically up and down river, searching for food, and because the adults have no territory to defend they are less aggressive than breeding pairs.

Mallard are also ever-present along many lowland rivers and are easily spotted – particularly the green-headed males, or drakes, resplendent in their breeding plumage, which is seen at its best when lit up from below by winter sunlight reflected from ice.

Shyer or rarer species may be less easily seen, but are well worth looking out for. The slower, deeper, more lake-like reaches may attract tufted

A lowland river in the dead of winter has a special charm, the sparkling tracery of ice and snow highlighting the stream's meandering course through the chilly countryside.

duck or pochard, both species that feed by diving, rather than dabbling from the surface like the mallard. Some northern and western rivers are exploited by the fish-eating red-breasted merganser and the related goosander. The graceful great crested grebe and its relative the dumpy little grebe may also occasionally be seen in winter.

Coots and moorhens

Other water birds feed alongside waterfowl. The most numerous are often the coot and moorhen, which are both mostly black and look similar at a distance. However, coots are bulkier and spend more of their time swimming in the open water where they dive for food, and may form large flocks. A coot has a white shield on its face above its bill, and long, lobed toes to propel it through the water. The moorhen is smaller and more solitary, and more likely to be seen feeding on the bank before it dives for cover among the vegetation. It has a red shield on its forehead, a red and yellow bill, a ragged white line along each flank and white flashes on its tail.

In flight, the kingfisher reveals its glorious electric blue back and tail feathers. It flies so fast that it looks like a streak of blue light flashing along the river.

Moorhens are cautious birds, but not as wary as the grey herons that stand sentinel in the shallows, watching for fish. At the first glimpse of an intruder the average heron is likely to lift off with powerful flaps of its broad, arched wings and fly off up or down the river, or away over a fence and down into a concealed drainage ditch. Sometimes it is possible to catch a heron unawares and watch as it stalks and then impales its prey with a lightning stab of its spear-like bill, before flicking it around headfirst to swallow it whole. Hard winters can pose serious problems for herons, because thick ice makes fishing impossible, and birds that cannot find open water may die of starvation.

Kingfisher blue

Kingfishers may suffer the same problem. Some move downriver to tidal waters that do not freeze, but many others stay behind on lowland rivers if the season is not too icy.

Despite their vivid colours they can be surprisingly hard to spot, because they spend long periods sitting perfectly still on perches overhanging the water, often in the shade of trees or shrubs, watching and waiting for their prey. A kingfisher is more likely to be seen as a fleeting impression of electric blue and orange as it streaks rapidly up or down the river, keeping close to the water surface and vanishing round the next bend. One trick is to listen out for its loud, high-pitched, shrill whistle, nearly always uttered when the bird is alarmed into sudden flight. Sometimes the kingfisher will land on a perch within sight, providing a close view – with binoculars – of its dazzlingly beautiful plumage.

WATER VOLE

Thanks to its immortalisation as 'Ratty' in *The Wind in the Willows*, the water vole is, for many, the symbol of the wild river bank. The role is appropriate because water voles – which are definitely not rats – need muddy river banks and relatively unpolluted water, so their presence is an indicator of an unspoilt, healthy river. Since they are active by day there is a fairly good chance of seeing one if the habitat is suitable, although these creatures are now scarce.

Water voles eat riverside plants and excavate their burrows in the banks. A close look at a river's muddy banks may reveal neat holes at or near the water surface, which may be the entrances to water vole burrows. A telltale sign that voles are about is an area of closely grazed vegetation near the holes. There may also be a pile of pith or pieces of bark left over after a vole has finished feeding. Wait quietly, and a distinct 'plop' may indicate that a vole has dived into the water. It swims with most of its body submerged.

This chestnut coloured rodent has small ears and beady eyes. It tends to eat just the juiciest parts of waterside plants, but often grazes a patch of the river bank until there is nothing left.

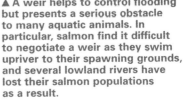

▲ A weir helps to control flooding but presents a serious obstacle to many aquatic animals. In particular, salmon find it difficult to negotiate a weir as they swim upriver to their spawning grounds, and several lowland rivers have lost their salmon populations as a result.

◄ Winter offers the best chance of seeing the secretive Cetti's warbler, because in summer it is usually hidden by the dense foliage of the thickets that it favours.

► Identifiable as a damselfly nymph by its three 'tails', this red damselfly is one of many insects that overwinter as larvae on the river bed.

Marshy ground close to the river also attracts waders such as redshank and snipe. These birds use their long bills to probe for small animals. Although wary, redshank are often relatively easy to see, but snipe have a habit of lying low until the last minute. They burst up from almost underfoot with a hoarse, ripping alarm call, then fly off, zigzagging rapidly away.

The wildlife of the riverside is always more varied where trees have been allowed to grow. Willows and alders thrive in the moist, fertile soil, as do the poplars that are often planted near rivers. They all provide valuable shelter for wildlife. The fruits of the alder, which form small, dark cones in winter, attract mixed flocks of siskins and redpolls to feed on the seeds. These little finches are very acrobatic birds, and often dangle upside down from the tips of twigs like blue tits at a birdfeeder.

Explosive calls

Many of the smaller birds so typical of riversides in summer are migrants that spend their winters in the tropics. This includes most of the warblers, insect-eaters which are forced to migrate to find food. One riverside warbler remains, however – the scarce, skulking Cetti's warbler. Found only in southern and eastern England, where it has bred in small numbers since the early 1970s, this elusive, greyish brown bird is extremely difficult to see clearly, but betrays its presence with loud, almost explosive calls. These can be heard throughout the winter in scrubby willow thickets and riverside reedbeds, as can the male's brief but even louder, staccato song.

The River Nene, near Peterborough, is a rewarding place for watching wildfowl and birds of prey in winter.

▲ Often to be seen fishing on broad rivers in winter, the great crested grebe remains an elegant bird even without its spectacular breeding plumage.

▲ A grey wagtail may be seen at any time of year, picking food from the mud at the river's edge. Bold and distinctive, these long-tailed birds often draw attention with their shrill 'tziz-eet' flight calls.

▶ A little grebe, or dabchick, may be encountered on the river in winter. If it is disturbed, it is likely to vanish beneath the water's surface.

Another small riverside bird that stays on throughout the winter is the reed bunting. In summer the male is easily identifiable by his bold black head and white collar, but in winter both sexes look brown, streaky and rather sparrow-like, although the male still has a darker head than the female. Reed buntings tend to congregate in communal roosts in winter, often in reedbeds and other riverside vegetation. The largest of these roosts can contain several hundred birds, but such gatherings are becoming less common owing to a major decline from 1975 to 1999 in which some populations have dwindled by up to 68 per cent.

The slender grey wagtail is seldom seen far from water. It nests near fast-flowing upland streams, but in winter it moves to lowland rivers, favouring fast-flowing water near weirs and waterfalls. It is yellow below, which invites confusion with the smaller, daintier yellow wagtail, but the grey is the only one of the two that stays on for the winter.

Insect prey

The main reason why so many riverside birds disappear in winter is the relative scarcity of their insect prey. In spring and summer the air above the water is alive with midges, gnats and moths, which provide rich pickings for predatory dragonflies and damselflies. The cold weather kills off most of these flying insects, but a few stay airborne to provide prey for the bats that may emerge briefly in warm winter weather to hunt. Daubenton's bat is particularly

Wildfowl in winter

The winter months offer good opportunities for watching wildfowl on lowland rivers, especially in urban areas. Resident birds are far less secretive than during the breeding season, and their numbers and variety may be boosted by an influx of migrant birds from Europe and the Arctic. If the weather turns particularly cold, species that are usually associated with lakes may be forced to visit the flowing, largely ice-free waters of the river to find food.

The River Clyst in Devon, one of the feeder rivers of the Exe estuary, often attracts many birds in winter, including swans, mallards and coots as well as the inevitable gulls.

associated with rivers, and occasionally appears in the evening to hunt low over the water for moths and flies.

The larvae of many insects are aquatic and keep feeding below the water surface throughout the winter. These provide food for fish such as chub and bottom-feeding barbel in the southern half of Britain, as well as the more widespread grayling and the familiar brown trout. A surprising number of fish may be seen by simply walking quietly along the banks, and it may even be possible to see a pike lurking among the weeds near the river bank or at the edge of a deep pool. However, its dappled coloration makes this powerful predator difficult to spot unless it springs an ambush on a passing fish.

Another predatory fish worth looking out for is the perch, identifiable by the dark vertical bars on its flanks, spiny dorsal fin and orange lower fins. Young perch often form small shoals that lie among submerged tree roots, or around bridges and jetties. They become less gregarious with age, and the bigger specimens are, like the pike, solitary ambush hunters.

Hunting otters

All these fish, plus many others, make welcome prey for otters. Notoriously elusive and rare, especially on rivers that have a history of disturbance and pollution, this most charismatic of river animals is slowly re-colonising old haunts as improving water quality and recovering fish stocks enable its populations to build up after a long period of decline. It is active all year round, and indeed over most of Britain except the extreme north it even breeds at any time of year. Consequently, it hunts throughout the winter. It does so mainly at dusk or during the night, but anyone walking quietly down the bank of a fairly wild – but not necessarily remote – river on a dark winter's afternoon may well catch a glimpse of one swimming. An otter leaves a characteristic U-shaped ripple behind it, and a line of air bubbles. On frozen rivers, otters may hunt below the ice. They can stay submerged for at least four minutes, and when they do this their air bubbles stay trapped beneath the ice to chart their progress.

Otters need quite dense riverside cover if they are to breed – ideally thickets and old trees with plenty of holes around the roots in which they can construct their holts – so they are generally absent from rivers that have been tidied up to provide riverside facilities for humans. Despite this, they have been seen in some towns, so there is a chance of seeing one almost anywhere. However, many supposed otter sightings turn out to be glimpses of swimming mink. These animals are much smaller, darker and more widespread than otters, and careful identification is essential.

Architectural plants

Most of the soft-foliaged plants that live in or by the water die back in winter, but a few remain visible and even impressive throughout the year. Common reed and bulrush fade from green to straw yellow, but stay standing unless they are broken down by high winds or heavy snow. Their seed heads also persist through the colder months, with the feathery plumes of common reed creating a wonderful effect when backlit by low winter sun. The sturdier, cigar-like heads of bulrushes make convenient perches for small birds, such as reed buntings and stonechats. The arching foliage of sedges, such as the greater and lesser pond sedges and hairy sedge, may also survive to provide cover for riverside wildlife.

Two members of the carrot family are particularly associated with the riverside – the deadly hemlock, with its pretty feathery foliage in summer, and the enormous giant hogweed, which is also poisonous and can cause serious skin damage if touched. Giant hogweed is an alien plant introduced from south-east Europe, and generally considered a pest, but there is no denying its visual impact, even in winter.

Other common plants of the riverside include the balsams, one of which, Indian or Himalayan balsam, can still be seen in winter.

A river bank is a delight at any time of year, but on the right day, in the right light, a walk along a lowland river in winter can be a particular pleasure and well worth braving the cold to enjoy.

▲ Introduced Indian balsam is a common waterside plant. In dry weather its stems, bearing seed pods, persist into winter. The seeds germinate in spring.

◄ Bathed by the lime-rich waters of the chalk streams in which it grows, the submerged foliage of watercress stays green throughout the year.

WILDLIFE WATCH

Where can I see lowland river wildlife?

1 River Spey, Scottish Highlands
This famous river is dotted with splendid wildlife sites and flows through magnificent Highland scenery. Watch for the ospreys that return to the area from Africa in April to breed, and for whooper swans on the nearby freshwater marshes in winter. Goosanders and red-breasted mergansers can also be seen here. The rare white-faced darter dragonfly and northern damselfly are on the wing in summer.

2 River Tweed, Borders, Scotland
The tumbling waters of this salmon river are an ideal habitat for dippers and grey wagtails. Goosanders and oystercatchers can also be seen. Many of the river banks are wooded, adding to the beauty of the river, and increasing the diversity of wildlife. Watch for signs of mink, which are more easily seen than the native otters. The Tweed estuary has exciting winter wildfowl such as whooper and mute swans, and divers, grebes and goldeneye.

3 River Tees, Durham, Cleveland
This upland river runs close to fine woodland with red squirrels, and past important botanical sites including meadows with marsh orchids and ragged robin in summer, and river gravels with the rare shrubby cinquefoil. Other special flowers of the area include martagon lily, yellow star-of-Bethlehem and goldilocks buttercup. The bridge at Egglestone Abbey (Barnard Castle) has a colony of Daubenton's bats that hunt over the river in the warmer months. Teesmouth is an excellent spot to look for waders and wildfowl, especially in winter.

4 River Derwent catchment, North Yorkshire
The rivers feeding into the Derwent from the North York Moors are all well worth visiting. In parts of Farndale, for example, wild daffodils cover the river banks in a carpet of gold every spring. Dippers and water voles can also be spotted.

5 River Severn, Worcestershire, Shropshire
The Severn is one of Britain's finest lowland rivers, with wooded banks and tributaries and exciting wildlife, including otters, dippers, grey wagtails and kingfishers. The clean waters are home to salmon, trout, bullhead, stone loach and also crayfish in places. Summer dragonflies include the club-tailed dragonfly, white-legged damselfly and banded demoiselle.

6 Ouse Washes and Old Bedford River, Cambridgeshire
These grazed meadows lie between two watercourses, and are flooded in winter when they attract thousands of whooper and Bewick's swans. In the spring the wet meadows support breeding redshank, snipe and black-tailed godwits, while the spectacular male ruff may also be seen displaying. Dragonflies include the scarce chaser and hairy dragonfly.

7 River Nene, Cambridgeshire
The hay meadows flanking the River Nene are regularly flooded in winter to create the Nene Washes – a magnet to swans and ducks in winter, and an important breeding site in spring. The grasslands are rich in wildflowers in summer.

8 River Thames, Berkshire and Oxfordshire
The upper Thames has abundant wildlife, with kingfishers and grey wagtails, and many dragonflies and damselflies in summer. Some of the traditional water meadows have stands of fritillary in spring, notably in the grounds of Magdalen College, Oxford. The club-tailed dragonfly can be seen around Pangbourne.

9 River Kennet, Berkshire
This tributary of the Thames has some fine wildlife-watching sites, notably near Thatcham, where the river has an adjacent canal, gravel pits and reedbeds. Frequently seen birds include the great crested grebe and little grebe, water rail, grey wagtail, grey heron, sedge warbler and reed warbler.

10 River Wey, Surrey
Just 32km (20 miles) from London, the River Wey and its associated canal system act as a wildlife corridor through the heart of Surrey, flanked by water meadows and wet alder woods. It is an important breeding site for dragonflies.

11 River Dart, Devon
This fine river flows down from Dartmoor, opening out into a majestic estuary before entering the sea at Dartmouth. It supports a healthy fish fauna, including trout, salmon and eel. Upland birds include ring ouzels in summer, with dipper along the river. Watch for signs of otters. Siskins and crossbills can be seen in nearby plantations.

12 River Stour, Dorset
This is a good place to see grey herons and kingfishers. Summer dragonflies include white-legged, blue-tailed, large red and azure damselflies, scarce and broad-bodied chasers, the emperor dragonfly and southern hawker.

13 River Great Stour, Kent
The Great Stour is especially good at Stodmarsh near Canterbury. Here the riverside marshes have large reedbeds and grazed meadows, with reed warbler, sedge warbler, Cetti's warbler, the rare Savi's warbler and bearded tit. The meadows have snipe, redshank and, in spring and summer, garganey. In winter, they also have golden plovers and hen harriers.

14 River Fowey, Cornwall
The Fowey has abundant caddis flies and stoneflies, and as a result it is a famous trout river. It is also a haunt of the dipper and grey wagtail. Buzzards and sparrowhawks are common in the riverside woodland. The damp rocks support ferns, mosses and liverworts. Filmy ferns are a speciality.

15 River Shannon, Ireland
Ireland's longest river repays a visit for its wildlife, especially in the Shannonbridge area. Nearby winter-flooded meadows attract wintering Greenland white-fronted geese, whooper swans and Bewick's swans. Breeding corncrakes are there in summer.

One of southern England's most beautiful rivers, the Wey encompasses several nature reserves, which provide tranquil havens for wildlife.

Where rivers meet the sea

Constantly changing muddy estuaries are packed with tiny creatures that have adapted to the special conditions. They sift a living from the brackish water while salmon and eels linger to adjust to the saltiness on their journeys to the sea.

The meeting of fresh and salt water in estuaries creates a dynamic environment where conditions change from hour to hour through the day, and from month to month and season to season. In winter, they are especially dramatic, because they attract vast flocks of coastal birds that move south and west from northern Europe to take advantage of the milder Atlantic weather and the rich pickings to be found on the intertidal mud. As a result, estuaries around the British coastline are of international importance for nature conservation.

Tidal waters

An estuary is made by the ebb and flow of the tide, and its effect on the river flowing down to the sea. Twice a day the salty tide rushes in, pushing the fresh river water back upstream and filling the estuary to its banks. This stops the river in its tracks, allowing suspended silt and other particles to sink and settle on the bottom. When the tide turns and the water drains away, these sediments are revealed as great expanses of glistening mudflats, flanking a channel that is reduced to a much narrower, relatively fast-flowing stream. The bed of this channel is often stony, all the fine material having been scoured out by the current.

Some estuaries have been formed in more complex ways. After the last Ice Age, rising sea levels flooded coastal valleys around much of the British coastline, forming branching patterns of drowned valleys. Some of the finest of these are to be found in south-western England and western Scotland. In other areas the land has risen, elevating former river beds above sea level to form a series of raised river terraces, such as those along the course of the Thames estuary. Regardless of how they are formed, however, all estuaries are characterised by the same set of difficult environmental conditions.

Rise and fall

Both the estuary and its wildlife are in a state of constant flux. As the tide rises the current flows inland, carrying a fresh supply of nutrients from the sea. The incoming seawater also increases the saltiness, or salinity, of the water at any point in the estuary. The salt encourages fine silt grains to stick together, forming bigger particles – a process called flocculation – and this makes them more likely to settle as mudflats.

The depth of water steadily increases over a six-hour period, then stops at high tide, or high water. The extra-high 'spring tides' that occur twice a month flood the estuary from shore to shore. Shortly after high water, the level begins to fall and the current reverses, becoming stronger and stronger as the water drains away. The currents of the falling tide are normally stronger than those of a rising tide, because of the additional flow from the river that feeds the estuary. This can be quite

▲ Common shrimps have semi-transparent bodies and are difficult to see in the murky waters of estuaries. However, they are readily detected by hungry flatfish, bass and mullet.

◄ Large shoals of sand-eels are found in most estuaries. They provide plenty of food for large fish as well as birds.

considerable if the river is a large one, such as the Thames or Severn. Small creatures are likely to be swept out of the estuary and into the sea unless they can swim against the current, or avoid it by burrowing into the mud.

Mud and salt

The clarity of the water in an estuary can vary greatly. The silt suspended in the river water can make it very cloudy. The scouring action of the tidal streams also stirs up sediment from the bed of the estuary, which adds to the murkiness of the water. This hampers the growth of submerged plants and algae, which need light to survive, but the silt is usually rich in nutrients that support vast numbers of burrowing molluscs, worms and other invertebrates. These in turn provide food for fish and coastal birds.

These burrowing animals must be able to tolerate not only the rise and fall of the tide, but the twice-daily fluctuations in salinity. The

WINTER WADERS

The estuaries of the British coastline support huge numbers of waders and other birds in winter. Many are Arctic breeders that have fled the cold northern weather, while others make shorter journeys from the British uplands. Many are just passing through, on their way to warmer climates.

In most estuaries there is plenty of food for all, and the birds exploit it using a variety of feeding methods. The shape and length of the bill determines the prey that each species can catch. For instance, busy flocks

of dunlin use their medium-length bills to snatch small animals from the surface or to probe a short way into the mud. The greenshank, with its longer bill and legs, can wade in shallow water to pursue shrimps and small fish.

The oystercatcher uses its bright red bill to chisel open cockles or mussels, or probe the mud for lugworms. Grey and ringed plovers run over the mud, stopping and tilting forward to snap up small animals from the surface with their short, strong bills.

▲ A greenshank scours the shallows for food. These birds can be seen regularly on British estuaries, especially in the west.

◄ Using its big eyes, a grey plover scans for the slightest movement of prey on the banks of an estuary.

▼ The Exe estuary in south Devon – seen here near Turf – is one of the largest in Britain. It attracts Brent geese and many waders in winter.

DANGER!

● The tide can rise very rapidly in estuaries, so avoid visiting any areas where it is possible to get cut off. Always check the local tide tables before setting off. Don't go out on the tidal areas of an estuary on your own.

● Estuaries have extensive areas of soft, deep mud that can be treacherous, so do not attempt to walk on them.

● The channels left at low tide can be very deep, with strong currents, so do not try to wade across them.

● Look for special nature reserve areas or visitor centres where you can seek advice about the best areas to visit safely – and avoid disturbing breeding or overwintering birds.

salinity of sea water is fairly constant at around 35 parts per thousand of dissolved salts, but in an estuary the salinity can vary with the state of the tide. This is a problem for many marine animals, because their body fluids have a salt balance that is normally adapted for life in seawater. If they enter freshwater, their salty bodies are likely to absorb water in an attempt to redress the balance, by a process called osmosis, and this can be fatal.

Estuarine animals have to be able to overcome this problem, and so do migrant fish such as eels and salmon, which spend part of their lives in freshwater lakes and rivers and the rest at sea. Salmon spawn in clear, gravelly upland streams. At an early stage in

their lives the young fish migrate downriver and pass through estuaries to the sea, where they feed on a diet of marine fish and crustaceans. Many travel as far as the rich feeding grounds of the Davis Strait off the western coast of Greenland. Some years later they return to spawn, so each fish makes at least two trips through an estuary. The fish often spend some time in the tidal estuary, and this helps them to acclimatise to the change in salinity before continuing their journey.

Epic journey
Freshwater eels make similar journeys, but in reverse. They swim up estuaries when they are tiny elvers – virtually transparent, thread-like creatures with large dark eyes. The elvers migrate in shoals that are carried into estuaries on the flood tide, and they eventually find their way into freshwater rivers, often during autumn floods. Huge numbers

are caught by commercial elver fishermen, either as a culinary delicacy – most of the catch is now exported to Europe or China – or for restocking ponds and lakes that the eels cannot reach on their own. The main elver fisheries are in the Severn and other rivers draining into the Bristol Channel, and in parts of East Anglia, but far fewer are caught now than in the past, owing to a serious decline in eel stocks in both Britain and Europe.

On reaching fresh water, the surviving elvers continue their epic journey up rivers and streams, and even overland across muddy ground, until they reach suitable places to settle. They feed and grow for several years, until the urge to migrate strikes again, and they begin the long return journey downriver to the estuary.

Here they spend some time during late autumn and early winter, acclimatising to salt water. The variable salinity of the estuary enables them to make the transition in easy stages. Eventually they swim out to sea and embark on a long journey across the ocean to the depths of the Sargasso Sea in mid-Atlantic.

Despite being a marine creature, the shore crab is able to scavenge on the mudflats at low tide. However, these crabs make easy targets for predatory birds if they cannot hide under stones or debris.

Brent geese are non-breeding winter visitors to British estuaries from their Arctic nesting grounds. Flocks arrive from September and remain until March. This is the smallest, regularly seen goose in Britain, recognisable by its mostly dark plumage, white collar and stern.

TEEMING MUDFLATS

Estuaries that are fed by large rivers or have unusually slack currents often build up very extensive banks of deep mud. These make perfect habitats for burrowing worms, molluscs, crustaceans and other invertebrates. The variety of species is not very great when compared with those found on sandy beaches, because the variations in salinity and the airless nature of the mud make life difficult for most marine animals. However, the enormous amount of food available enables tolerant species to thrive in vast numbers. One survey of buried molluscs in a tidal bank of muddy sand revealed 2000 common cockles in a single square metre (11 sq ft).

A cockle lies partly buried in the sand, its shells gaping slightly open when it is covered by water. This allows it to extend a short tube, called an inhalant siphon, to draw water into its body. The water is filtered to strain off any food, and passed through the gills to absorb oxygen. The waste water is expelled through a second (exhalant) siphon. The cockle's tough shell protects it from most predators, but crabs, some very large fish and a few birds, such as the oystercatcher, can open the shell. Gulls sometimes pick up cockles in their bills, fly up and drop them on rocks to crack them open.

The peppery furrow shell also extends two very long siphons up through the mud to the surface. The longer siphon sweeps over the surface in search of food, drawing it in with a current of water, and in the process making star-like radiating lines in the mud. The shorter siphon acts as a waste water outlet.

In the most sheltered backwaters of the estuary, where the mud is covered with a fine layer of algae, there will be an abundance of tiny *Hydrobia* snails, or laver spire shells. These diminutive grazing molluscs are sometimes so common that handfuls of the rice-grain sized shells can be scooped up from the line of the high tide, called the strand line. They are a vital source of food for many birds, especially ducks, particularly shelducks, and waders, such as knots and sanderlings.

Several marine worms, including lugworms and ragworms, live in and on mudflats. Ragworms are the more active of these two species, sometimes emerging from their burrows to swim in search of food. Both kinds of worm are relished by birds, but only the curlew or whimbrel, with their very long down-curved bills, or the godwits with their almost equally long straight bills, can reach them in the mud.

► One of the most common molluscs that lives in estuarine mud, the peppery furrow shell usually buries itself vertically. If it feels threatened it swiftly retracts its two siphons.

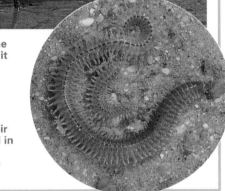

▲ The long, black bill of the curlew sandpiper enables it to probe the mudflats for invertebrates buried well beneath the surface.

► Ragworms are active predators that burrow their way through silt and sand in search of prey. They are sometimes found beneath stones at low tide.

At low water the river is often reduced to a fast-flowing, narrow channel carved through deep banks of wet, sticky mud. As the tide floods in again, the whole estuary is transformed into a broad sheet of water.

Once they reach their destination, the eels spawn and die. Their eggs hatch into tiny larvae that drift back east across the Atlantic, becoming elvers just in time to begin their upriver migration.

Lying low

Some fish spend much of their lives in estuaries. The flounder is very well adapted to this environment, with a high tolerance for changes of salinity, a flattened body that enables it to lie on the bottom, and perfect camouflage that helps conceal it from predators. It preys on shore crabs, lugworms, ragworms, small molluscs and small fish.

Flounders spend most of their time in estuarine and fresh waters, but they always migrate into the open sea to spawn. At low tide, flounders are confined to muddy creeks where they risk being caught by patiently stalking grey herons, or elegant, pure white little egrets, which have become increasingly common in southern Britain in recent years. They are also heavily preyed upon by cormorants.

The bass is an elegant, silvery fish with a spiny front dorsal fin. Large shoals of bass may come in with the flood tide to feed on small fish and invertebrates being swept along in the current. Estuaries act as important nursery areas for young bass. They are quite often found in tidal pools in the salt marshes that line estuaries, but they move into

deeper water in winter, and move out into the open sea to mature into adults.

One of several sand-eel species that form a vital link in the marine food chain, the small sand-eel is devoured in its millions by terns, kittiwakes, puffins and guillemots. They are not true eels, but small, elongated fish that live in vast shoals, and bury themselves in sandy sea beds for protection. Even here they may be taken by bass, or by diving birds, such as cormorants.

At first glance, an estuary can seem a bleak place, especially in winter when a cold wind is blowing in off the sea, but the flocks of birds that descend on them show that they are teeming with life. In fact, estuaries are among the most important of all marine habitats.

▲ In their first year of life, bass frequently venture into the more saline waters of estuaries. They are voracious predators of smaller fish, as well as crabs, shrimps, marine worms and other invertebrates.

▼ As a young flounder develops, it lies on its left side. Then its left eye migrates on to its right side, so it can still see with its body pressed flat against the bottom. Flounders grow up to 50cm (20in) long.

ALGAE AND PLANT LIFE

▲ At low tide, filamentous, irregularly constricted tubes of gutweed are often inflated with air.

The murky waters of most estuaries are not ideal for the growth of marine algae and plants. Many algae (seaweeds) are carried in and out of the estuary on the tide, but only a few can grow there, in shallow areas and where solid structures provide a secure base to which they can attach themselves.

One of the most common seaweeds able to tolerate estuarine conditions is gutweed, which gets its name because it looks like strands of green intestine. It forms dense masses where streams of fresh water trickle over mud or rocks.

Bladder wrack, a brown seaweed, can also survive near the mouth of an estuary where there is enough current to keep silt levels low.

Eelgrasses are flowering plants that grow submerged in the shallows in muddier areas. In the most sheltered places they give way to salt-tolerant vegetation that is characteristic of a salt marsh, such as glasswort and sea purslane.

Seaweeds provide food for many animals, as well as sheltering invertebrates, such as sandhoppers, on which birds feed. Eelgrasses attract winter-visiting brent geese and wigeon, for which they are a major food.

► The shifting sediment layer of an estuary is no place for most seaweeds, but jetties or the wooden posts of breakwaters are swiftly colonised by species such as bladder wrack.

WILDLIFE WATCH

Where can I visit estuaries ?

1 Holy Island, Northumberland
A very large area of sheltered sand and mudflats is protected from the open sea by Holy Island. Only a small amount of fresh water enters this area, so the water is clear and currents are slow. The site is very important for both breeding and overwintering birds, and especially rich in invertebrates. Nearby is Budle Bay, another very sheltered area, also favoured by overwintering birds.

2 Solway Firth
A vast area of tidal flats, river channels, creeks and salt marshes, the Solway Firth divides England from Scotland. It attracts many overwintering wildfowl (especially geese) and waders, and is home to important populations of fish and invertebrates.

3 Morecambe Bay, Cumbria
Famed for its overwintering birds, the second largest bay in Britain also supports fisheries and has masses of molluscs and marine worms in its extensive mudflats and sand banks.

4 Dee and Mersey estuaries
Together, these estuaries form a huge complex of mudflats, sand banks and tidal channels. Although once heavily polluted in places, they are now increasingly important for wintering birds and breeding gulls, terns and waders.

5 The Humber estuary, Humberside
Large areas of industrial land and several docks and harbours border this estuary, which has the long sand spit of Spurn Head at its mouth. The whole area is host to a large number of overwintering and migrant birds. Recent storms and high tides have seriously eroded the sand spit, turning Spurn Head into an island.

6 The Wash, East Anglia
The Wash is a vast area of mudflats, sand banks and salt marshes, surrounded by low-lying fenland. Internationally important populations of waders and wildfowl overwinter here, and large numbers of gulls, terns and waders breed in the summer. Common seals also use the sand banks.

7 Burry inlet, south Wales
Part of a larger complex of estuaries and mudflats, this area is noted for its molluscs, such as cockles, and its large bird populations.

8 Severn estuary, Bristol Channel
The Severn is the principal river entering this great estuary, but many others, such as the Wye, Usk and Avon, also flow into it. They bear large loads of silt, which are deposited to form fertile mud banks where wintering birds feed. The 'Severn Bore' is an impressive tidal surge that rushes up the river for many miles when there are very high tides. The estuary is home to many fish as well as other marine organisms. It is also the site of Slimbridge, the headquarters of the Wildfowl & Wetland Trust, which is excellent for wintering geese as well as other wildfowl and waders.

9 Exe estuary, south Devon
The estuary of the River Exe has the port of Exmouth at its mouth and the historic city of Exeter at its head. It is the largest estuary in the south-west peninsula, and in winter it supports large numbers of wading birds, including avocets and oystercatchers. There is also a large winter population of Brent geese. The mouth of the estuary is sheltered by the long sand spit of Dawlish Warren.

10 Pagham Harbour, West Sussex
One of the few undeveloped parts of the Sussex coastline, Pagham is a large expanse of mud and salt marsh with important wintering flocks of waders and wildfowl, and colonies of breeding terns and waders in summer.

11 Thames estuary
Although heavily industrialised in places, there are still many quiet and protected stretches where wildlife can flourish. The tidal stretch penetrates into the heart of London, bringing birds and other wildlife within easy reach of the capital.

Estuaries form wherever river meets sea, and sites are located all around the coast. Some of the best ones to visit are listed here.

Cut off by the sea at high tide, Holy Island in Northumberland reveals a huge expanse of sheltered estuarine mudflats as the waters recede.

Dawlish Warren, at the mouth of the Exe estuary, is a haven for wildlife. At high tide, large numbers of birds roost here, including oystercatchers and increasing numbers of little egrets.

Sandy shore – life underfoot

In the wet and shiny sand of a beach at low tide, thousands of marine organisms lie buried. They leave the minutest of traces on the surface as they descend into the relative safety of their burrows.

A beach in winter can be a violent and even dangerous place. Whipped up by seasonal gales, great grey waves roll in, topple and break upon the sand, to surge up the shore and sluice back beneath the next incoming wave. The beach is a scene of desolation, littered with debris – much of it the remains of dead animals. It often looks like the aftermath of some natural disaster.

Beneath the surface, however, lies a different world. The sand is alive with animals living safely and comfortably in their burrows, insulated from the swirling turmoil above. Clues to some of this hidden life can be seen at low tide. The familiar casts of lugworms indicate the living animals beneath, small pits show where razorshells have burrowed, and star-shaped holes mark the presence of heart-urchins. Standing up above the sand are the ragged tubes of sand mason worms, looking like ill-used artists' brushes, and sometimes the drinking-straw tubes of other burrowing worms. The high-water mark, or strand line, at the top of the beach contains the shells of many other creatures swept up from the lower shore, including those of bivalve molluscs such as tellins, venus shells and razorshells, as well as the empty sandy tubes of burrowing worms. Occasionally, starfish and brittlestars may be stranded in shallow pools.

Coping with sand

The sand presents beach burrowers with some fundamental problems. First, they must have some way of obtaining food and oxygen from the water above at high tide. Second, they must get rid of their waste so that it does not foul their burrows. Third, they must ensure that their offspring can reach the open sea, and disperse along the coast to spread the species.

These requirements mean that all the animals must maintain some sort of link with the seawater above, in the form of a passage that is kept open either temporarily or permanently. At low tide, these links are the main clues to the animals' presence. Most of them do not stay open as the tide recedes, but they leave traces on the sand.

The most obvious of these traces are the coiled casts of lugworms, each of which marks the end of a U-shaped burrow in the sand. The cast is made of sand that has passed

▲ Rarely seen out of its burrow, a lugworm has a muscular body equipped with feathery red gills for absorbing vital oxygen from the water.

▼ Herring gulls are sharp-eyed opportunists that rarely miss a chance for an easy meal, and make short work of any exposed beach animals they find.

through the worm's gut, because it feeds by drawing surface sand down from the other end of the burrow into its mouth. It strips the sand of any digestible organic detritus, as well as most of the bacteria that is feeding on the detritus, and ejects the stripped sand from the other end of the burrow to form the cast. The worm lies deep enough to be beyond the reach of most predators except very long-billed waders, such as the curlew.

Predatory worm

Unlike the lugworm, the common ragworm lives in a temporary burrow, and spends much of its time out on the surface of the sand, even at low tide. It is an active hunter and can move about over the sediment with the aid of numerous leg-like structures called parapodia.

The ragworm locates small crustaceans and other prey with its sensitive antennae and two pairs of eyes, and then seizes them with its strong,

black, pincer-like jaws. In turn, it is a favourite prey of many wading birds, which are often able to pick it off the surface of the sand.

The efficiency of the ragworm's parapodia is enhanced by many retractable bristles called chaetae. Lugworms and ragworms are classed as polychaetes, because they have large numbers of chaetae. They are also known more descriptively as bristleworms. In some polychaetes all the segments

are similar, but in others, including lugworms, the body is divided into regions that have different functions, such as respiration, reproduction and excretion.

Many other species of polychaete worms inhabit the sandy shore. Most of them make temporary burrows in the sand, like the ragworm, but others construct various types of projecting tubes. One species, the sand mason, is especially skilled at this. Selecting individual sand

BURROWING BRITTLESTAR

The brittlestars are well named, because their slender arms break off easily. However, a damaged arm can be regenerated, unlike the central disc. By burrowing beneath the surface, the long-armed brittlestar protects its vulnerable central disc, leaving just the tips of four of its five arms exposed at the surface. The arms generate a current that draws tiny food particles into the animal's burrow. These are ingested through an opening on the underside of the disc. Its gut is a simple bag, and indigestible matter is forced out the same way it goes in.

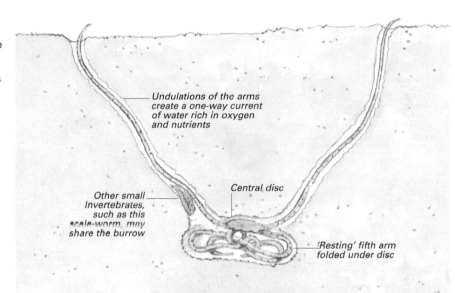

Undulations of the arms create a one-way current of water rich in oxygen and nutrients

Other small Invertebrates, such as this scale-worm, may share the burrow

Central disc

'Resting' fifth arm folded under disc

The arms of brittlestars are flexible and very mobile, but also fragile, so it is best to leave the animals well alone.

Common brittlestars may live in shallow pools in the sand, but if they are stranded by the receding tide they must stay hidden to avoid being snapped up by gulls. When the tide comes in again, they are free to extend their feathery arms in the water to collect drifting particles of food.

grains, it cements them together in just the right position, first to build the tube itself, then to make a bunch of hairs at the top end of the tube. These act as a snare to catch planktonic organisms, which the worm then 'licks' off with its tentacles.

Another species, the peacock worm, constructs a similar but simpler tube from finer material, with no hair-like structures. It lives in colonies, which at low tide look like muddy macaroni embedded in the shore. At high tide, however, the worm reveals the reason for its name by extending a crown of multi-coloured feathery tentacles, and expanding them like a fan in the water. The tentacles – which are modified gills – absorb oxygen and trap suspended particles, passing them to the centre of the fan to be either eaten or used to maintain the tube.

The tentacles are extremely sensitive, and withdrawn at the slightest alarm.

Buried bivalves

The most accomplished beach burrowers are bivalve molluscs, such as the various clams. Their hinged shells, or valves, protect their bodies from both abrasion and attack, so they can survive the dangers of the tidal beach.

The five British species of razorshell are among the most efficient burrowers. Each razorshell has a powerful foot with which it can move up or down its deep vertical burrow. It normally positions itself fairly near the sand surface with its two siphon tubes protruding, so it can draw water containing food and oxygen down one tube, and void waste from the other. If it senses danger, it closes its shells and quickly pulls itself downwards, out of trouble. This action is often

accompanied by a jet of water that squirts up from the burrow.

The beaches along the south and west coasts of Britain may harbour huge populations of one of the most interesting burrowers, the common heart-urchin or sea potato. This animal is a relative of the spiny sea urchins but it feels furry to the touch because most of its very fine spines lie flat against the surface of its body. Some of the spines on the underside are mobile and somewhat

paddle-shaped. These take the major role in burrowing, scraping sand from the animal's front end and shifting it to the rear.

Heart-urchins live 5–20cm (2–8in) below the surface. Each maintains contact with the water above with the long, hydraulic tube-feet that protrude from its upper surface. The urchin extends these upwards to excavate a narrow tubular funnel to the surface. As each tube-foot moves up and down it plasters sticky mucus on to the sand

Eelgrasses are not seaweeds, but true flowering plants with leaves, roots and tiny flowers, like land plants. The three British species are restricted to very sheltered shores.

A bed of eelgrass helps to consolidate beach sand and mud. It provides shelter for many animals, but few creatures eat it apart from geese and sea urchins.

SHARING A BURROW

The beach burrow of a common heart-urchin, and particularly its rear-facing soakaway, may attract a number of extra residents. One of these is a tiny rust-coloured bivalve mollusc called Montacute's shell. Since it is no more than 4mm (⅙in) long it takes up little space, and three or four of these animals may live in one burrow, attached to the urchin by the same type of structure that mussels use to attach themselves to rocks, called a byssus thread. If an urchin is removed from its burrow it may have several of these creatures hanging from its rear end. They enjoy a steady food supply and a safe refuge, and in return help to keep the burrow free from waste.

▼ Heart-urchins burrow out of sight into the sand. Often there is no obvious sign of their presence, even on beaches where they are common.

◄ Living heart-urchins are covered with very short spines that feel soft to the touch. Their bodies display the five-rayed pattern found in all echinoderms, but most obvious in starfishes.

Dunnet Beach, Caithness, in Scotland, is a typical sandy shore, scoured clean by the tide twice a day.

walls to prevent collapse. Once the funnel has been created, minute hair-like cilia on the urchin's body beat in concert to produce a steady current of water down to the animal. This goes on even when the tide is out, because water usually remains in the burrow, enabling the tube-feet and cilia to maintain the funnel and downward current.

Another set of tube-feet project from the rear end of the body to build and maintain a horizontal tube extending for about 10cm (4in) behind the animal. The current bringing water down the funnel to the burrow continues into this tube, carrying away any waste.

It is possible to excavate a heart-urchin and gently lift it out to examine it briefly. When it is put back on the sand it starts to burrow by shovelling sand out to its sides.

The front end tips downwards, and within about 20 minutes the animal has disappeared.

Spines and tubes

Heart-urchins belong to a group of invertebrates called echinoderms, which means 'spiny-skinned'. These include not only the sea urchins but also starfishes, brittlestars and sea cucumbers. They are among the most successful marine animals – a success that is due principally to their remarkable tube-feet. The ends of these are modified for the special functions they perform, like the attachments

on a vacuum-cleaner hose. They may be either pointed for use as feelers, rounded for respiration, feathery for picking up sand and applying mucus to the burrow walls, or equipped with suckers for handling food or clinging to hard surfaces.

The most familiar of these animals are the starfishes. Along with their relatives, the brittlestars, these usually have five arms, which are short and stumpy in starfishes but long, slender and very fragile in the brittlestars. The sand star lives on tidal beaches, burrowing a little way into the sand but

A characteristic inhabitant of sandy beaches, the sand star has a smooth upper surface with a fringe of creamy white spines. It burrows in the surface layers of sand, and usually grows to about 12cm (5in) across.

RAZORSHELL MOVEMENT

Like all burrowing bivalve molluscs, a razorshell burrows into the sand using a muscular, extendible 'foot'. The foot can be inflated with blood at its bottom end so it swells up and acts as an anchor, enabling the animal to haul itself down into the sand. The foot of a razorshell is particularly long and powerful, and works so

rapidly that the animal can disappear into its burrow almost instantly, aided by a jet of water that it blasts from its siphon tubes by slamming its shell valves shut. The foot also stops the shell being pulled out of its burrow easily, and the animal is likely to break in half rather than allow itself to be dragged into the open.

The razorshell owes its name to its resemblance to an old-fashioned cut-throat razor.

▲ An upended razorshell extends its inlet and outlet siphons. These allow it to feed and breathe while remaining safely hidden below the surface.

◄ The hinged shells, or valves, of a bivalve mollusc such as this cockle can open up, allowing the animal to extend its strong muscular 'foot'.

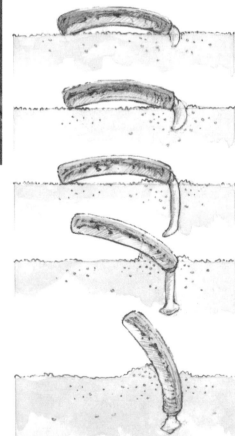

The razorshell starts to push its very large, muscular foot into the sand.

The foot extends and continues pushing downwards.

When it is deep enough, the foot tip is inflated with blood to grip the sand.

The foot contracts, drawing the shell down into the sand after it.

The process is rapidly repeated until the razorshell is safely hidden from sight.

The ringed plover is a common sight on many sandy and muddy beaches in winter on estuaries around the British Isles. Like most plovers, it has a distinctive, jerky run-stop-tilt feeding action.

keeping the tips of its arms and the top of its central disc just protruding. Like heart-urchins, it uses currents created by minute cilia to waft water containing food and oxygen towards its central mouth and gills.

Pumping arms

The burrowing long-armed brittlestar has a different way of keeping the all-important currents flowing past its gills and mouth. It lives at depths of about 1–10cm below the surface (½–4in), but with the tips of its arms protruding. Two of the five arms generate an inward current and one or two generate the outflow. This leaves a fifth arm unused, and curled up under the animal's central disc, as though resting. The reason for this is probably connected with mucus production. Burrowing uses a lot of mucus, which both maintains the burrow and protects the animal from sharp sand grains. The spare arm is probably left inactive to restock its mucus glands. Eventually another arm is withdrawn from pumping duty to take the place of the resting arm, and in this way each arm is given a chance to revive itself.

Sand stars and brittlestars are not nearly as common on sandy beaches as the other inhabitants, but they are sometimes chanced upon when they have come to the surface for some reason, such

WADERS FEEDING

During the autumn, many species of waders migrate to Britain from the Arctic because the winters are less severe. Even in very cold winter weather, the sandy shores on British coasts do not freeze up. Thousands of dunlins, sandpipers and knots form huge flocks that patiently sit out high tide, then follow the receding waterline down the beach seeking stranded shrimps, small fish and worms brought in by the sea, as well as tiny molluscs buried in the surface layers of the shore. Larger waders such as curlews and godwits probe the sand for worms, and oystercatchers smash open mussels and cockles. Some wader flocks may number many thousands, and resemble smoke when they all take flight at once, swirling and billowing through the air.

▲ With its smart black and white plumage, pink legs, big carrot-coloured bill and shrill calls, the oystercatcher is one of the most easily recognised of the waders.

▼ Sandy shores and muddy estuaries provide ideal hunting grounds for the bar-tailed godwit, seen here, and its longer-billed relative the black-tailed godwit.

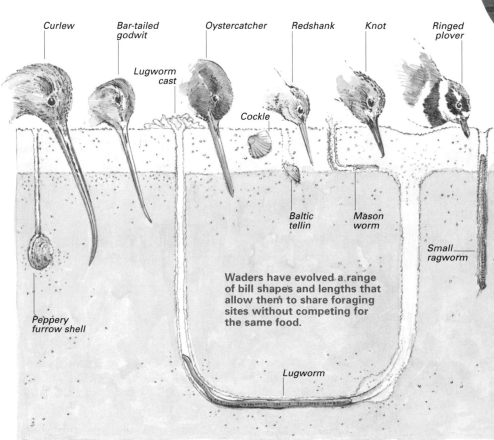

Curlew   Bar-tailed godwit   Oystercatcher   Redshank   Knot   Ringed plover

Lugworm cast

Cockle

Baltic tellin

Mason worm

Small ragworm

Peppery furrow shell

Waders have evolved a range of bill shapes and lengths that allow them to share foraging sites without competing for the same food.

Lugworm

Dunlins nest on moorland, but cannot remain there in winter when their food supply dwindles. They migrate to sandy shores, to feed on the animals revealed by falling tides.

as disturbance or lack of oxygen. Such exposures offer an opportunity to examine them closely, but like all beach animals they should not be touched.

Beach fish

Invertebrates are not the only animals making a living from the sand. When the tide is in, fish such as the sand goby and common goby mouth their way over the surface ripples to glean fragments of detritus.

When the tide goes out, the rippled sand can look virtually devoid of life. In fact, the whole beach is alive with animals that stay hidden beneath the surface until the water returns.

A walk along the water's edge as the tide drops may also disturb a sand-eel, which darts away in a brief flash of silver as it senses danger. These little fish are able to burrow into wet sand with terrific speed, using the same technique employed by the lugworm, razorshells and most other beach burrowers. Sand-eels are the staple diet of many seabirds, and if they become less abundant for some reason, such as overfishing or a lack of food caused by rising water temperatures, this can have a serious effect on the populations of birds that feed on the shore and in nearby shallow seas.

Seagrass beds

A receding spring tide – an extra-low tide that occurs twice a month – will sometimes reveal a bed of seagrass, bright green with fronds up to 50cm (20in) long and 4–10mm (½in) wide. This is one of the eelgrasses – the only British flowering plants that have managed to colonise the sea.

Its presence in shallow water offers opportunities for animals to settle on its fronds and burrow among its roots. One animal occasionally seen attached to eelgrass is the snakelocks anemone, which has long green and purple tentacles that are rarely withdrawn more than slightly into the body. Another spectacular settler is a tiny

stalked jellyfish called *Lucernaria* which, rather than pulsating through the water in the usual jellyfish fashion, lives attached by its stalk to the fronds of seaweed, and sometimes eelgrass.

Every sandy shore is unique. Local, seasonal and daily environmental conditions, including the composition of the sand, the size of the waves, and whether the tides bring planktonic larvae ready to settle and turn into adults, will affect the wildlife of every shore. Even in the depths of winter animals are to be found – a fact that is evident from the large numbers of shorebirds that forage on the beach at low tide. There is a lot to be said for following their example, and taking a walk along the tideline to see what the waves have swept in – and to check the sand for traces of the hidden life below.

A third of a million knots overwinter in Britain. They can be seen on big beaches such as those of Morecambe Bay, the Wash and the Thames estuary.

WILDLIFE WATCH

What can I see on sandy shores?

● Sandy beaches are distributed all around the British coast. Those of the west tend to lie between rocky headlands and their sand is large-grained and scoured clean by the tide. East coast beaches tend to have finer particles, grading into mud. Each type offers opportunities for different forms of life. Eelgrass and slipper limpets are more common on the east coast for example, and cup corals are restricted to the west.

● Heavy seas churn up the sand, displacing many worms, molluscs and other animals that are normally buried in the sand. Look for them after stormy weather and exceptional tides.

● Some sandy shores are swept clean by the tides every day, but on others all sorts of marine debris can be found, especially after storms. Seaweeds, crabs, starfishes, masked crabs and many other organisms will be cast up on such shores.

● Most sandy shore animals can be seen alive only by digging them up. This exposes them to the air and predators, and in many cases the creatures cannot dig themselves back in again. They are better off left alone.

Strand line wildlife

Straggling lines of seaweed, shells and other debris left by the high tide are colonised by insects, which are eagerly sought by overwintering birds. They, in turn, are joined by mammals, such as foxes and otters, all scavenging for food.

The winter storms that batter the coasts of Britain toss all kinds of debris high up the shore, especially on sandy beaches and shingle banks. This mass of stranded material usually forms a distinct zone at the top of the beach, called the strand line.

The rising tide pushes up the shore twice a day but twice every month, at the times of the new and full moon, the gravitational pull of the moon on the sea is combined with the pull of the sun to cause an extra-high spring tide. This carries detritus even higher up the shore. After each spring tide has passed, the high tides over the following week cover less and less of the shore, leaving their debris lower down each day. This can create a series of strand lines along the beach.

After the neap tide – the lowest high tide, which occurs at every half moon – the high-tide level starts to creep back up again. It rises a little higher each day, sweeping all the separate strand lines back into one big, elongated heap. A major storm can sometimes wash everything away, but the next high tide will create another strand line.

Beachcombing

Much of the material that is deposited twice daily by the tide will be seaweeds, empty shells, egg cases and the remains of dead marine

◀ The tiny lesser white-toothed shrew, found only on the Isles of Scilly, forages along the strand line for small invertebrates.

▶ Decaying seaweeds on the strand line are the breeding habitat of kelp flies. These insects lay their eggs in the weed, and the larvae feed on it.

organisms. Other items that end up on the shore include driftwood and, sadly, rubbish of various kinds.

An extraordinary variety of objects are to be found on the strand line, accounting for the fascination of beachcombing. Most of the shells that are washed up will be those of native marine molluscs, but sometimes they are the remains of animals that have come from much farther away. Most marine molluscs produce tiny, free-swimming larvae, which are carried by the current until they metamorphose into miniature adults. Sometimes these get carried far beyond their normal range, and so the occasional mollusc from the West Indies or the coast of West Africa finds its way on to a Cornish beach.

▲ Organic debris found on the strand line is often alive with sandhoppers. They dry out easily, so they rarely venture out of their damp retreat.

▼ Successively lower high tides may leave several strand lines, such as these on the beach at Snettisham, Norfolk.

BEACH LAW

Much of the foreshore on the British coast is Crown property with free public access. Collecting natural debris is perfectly legal, but some shellfish, such as oysters, may be farmed and so gathering them is prohibited. Shipwrecks and valuable objects will also belong to someone. Beached whales, dolphins and porpoises are regarded in law as 'royal fish' (despite being mammals). For guidelines about what can be taken from the shore, contact the local coastguard, the police or the Receiver of Wreck (a department of the Maritime and Coastguard Agency).

FLOTSAM AND JETSAM

Beachcombing has been a traditional activity in Britain for so long that special words are used to describe some man-made objects found on the strand line. Anything that floats ashore after being lost from a wrecked ship is known as flotsam. Any items that are thrown overboard, or jettisoned, are called jetsam.

Many beaches are littered with rubbish, whether or not it originated on boats. Much of it is made of plastic, which is likely to remain for a long time unless the beach is cleaned. Glass or metal may be encrusted by seaweeds. Some of the rubbish can be deadly to wildlife. Seabirds and otters, for example, may drown if they get entangled in discarded fishing nets.

Seabirds may also be killed by oil at sea. Diving birds that spend much of their time on the water are most at risk, including divers, sea ducks and auks such as guillemots and razorbills. Oil-clogged feathers reduce buoyancy and insulation, so birds may drown or die of exposure, or of poisoning as they try to clean themselves.

◀ Driftwood may originate far from the shore where it eventually washes up, and the level of colonisation by barnacles, seaweeds and shipworms will indicate how long it has been in the sea.

The egg cases of dog whelks form the spongy, pale balls that are a common find among piles of knotted wrack on the strand line, especially in winter.

▶ Metal or glass objects, as well as pebbles, are often covered with sinuous, chalky tubes that were once the homes of tube worms.

At times, the strand line will be littered with thousands of empty shore-crab shells. These are the result of whole populations of crabs moulting and casting their outgrown shells simultaneously.

The egg cases of sharks, skates and rays are also common finds. Each of these flattened, leathery structures, known as 'mermaid's purses', protects a single embryonic fish as it develops inside, sustained by a supply of yolk. When the young fish emerges, the empty egg case finds its way to the shore.

Some of the seaweed-like materials dumped among the true seaweeds on the strand line are actually colonies of simple animals. Resembling a tough, horny, colourless seaweed, they are known as hornwrack. Close examination through a hand lens reveals that they are made up of numerous tiny chambers, and each of these once housed an individual organism.

Pieces of driftwood are often colonised by burrowing marine creatures such as the shipworm. A species of bivalve mollusc with a tiny shell and a worm-like body, the shipworm leaves long, twisting tunnels in the timber, which are lined with a white chalky material. Large numbers of small holes all over the surface of the wood are usually the work of the gribble, a tiny crustacean.

Seaweed feast

The great mass of seaweed dumped on many shores soon starts to rot down. As it does so it warms up and becomes easier to digest, providing a perfect habitat and food supply for the larvae of kelp flies. These flies are normally to be seen swarming all along the strand line. They lay their eggs on the rotting seaweed, and when the tiny, white larvae emerge from the eggs they immediately start to feed. They grow quickly on their nutritious diet, and develop into adults in just two weeks. Within days their own eggs will have hatched into a new generation of larvae.

Sand hoppers – small, flattened crustaceans that resemble freshwater shrimps – also live beneath the rotting seaweed, where they feed on small fragments of decaying matter. If the seaweed is disturbed they live up to their name, hopping wildly in every direction to escape.

In some regions, farmers and gardeners collect seaweed for use as a fertiliser and soil improver. It is rich in plant

Crabs have to moult their old shells as they grow, and the empty shells can often be found among the seaweed on the shore.

nutrients, particularly phosphates, and adds organic matter to the thin soils of many coastal areas. In the past, the largest kelps were collected and burnt in kelp pits on the coasts of Scotland and Ireland to provide a phosphate-rich ash. This was used as a fertiliser and in various industrial processes.

Rich pickings

The variety of edible material to be found on the strand line attracts expert beachcombers. Throughout the winter the turnstone – a stocky, active little wader – seeks out stranded periwinkles, sandhoppers and other invertebrates by using its short, powerful bill to flip over

small pebbles and pieces of seaweed in the most recent strand line. The blackish brown winter plumage on its back helps it to merge with its background and escape the notice of predators.

Rock pipits – which look rather like small long-legged, streaky thrushes – also search for small invertebrates, being especially good at catching adult kelp flies. During migration periods, resident rock pipits are joined by passing migrants such as wagtails, snow buntings and wheatears, which all appreciate a ready supply of food before continuing on their way. Lower down the shore, the little waders called sanderlings may be seen running along at the edge of the surf like clockwork toys, looking for tiny organisms being carried up the shore by the waves.

It is not only birds that take advantage of the food on offer. On some shores with nearby freshwater streams, especially in the northern isles and western parts of Scotland, Wales and Ireland, otters move quietly among the seaweeds and driftwood, searching for live fish and other animals to eat. Paw prints in the sand may also indicate the presence of foxes and rats, and less likely

Some of the most curious items to be washed up on the shore are the colonies of goose barnacles found attached to driftwood and other buoyant debris. They are crustaceans – relatives of shrimps – encased by thin, whitish shells on the ends of flexible stalks. Each has feather-like limbs folded up inside a shell, which it uses to gather food from the water.

The shell bears a slight resemblance to a bird's egg, and the lines on it look like a bird's folded wings. Long ago, this prompted the belief that they developed into the

Goose barnacles have shiny shells tinged with a purplish blue sheen. They are often found attached to debris washed up by the sea.

barnacle goose, a bird that was never seen to make a nest as it spends the breeding season in the High Arctic. It was suggested that a special tree grew on a distant shore, and the eggs were borne on the branches of this tree. Sometimes they fell into the sea and drifted to the shores of Britain, but those that remained grew feathers and became geese.

This was a popular notion in the Catholic Middle Ages, because it meant that the barnacle goose originated in the sea. It could be classified as fish, enabling it to be eaten on a Friday – a meat-free day for Catholics.

When submerged, goose barnacles extend their feather-like limbs to sweep the water for minute planktonic animals.

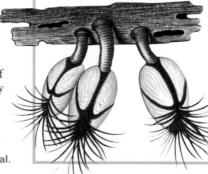

▲ A rock pipit patrols piles of rotting seaweed in search of small periwinkles and fly larvae. These birds pick the food off the surface with their slim bills.

▼ Foxes are opportunistic scavengers, and they soon discover the easy pickings on the strand line. Dead fish and crustaceans make a good meal.

▼ Tropical sea beans are sometimes found on beaches, especially in the south-west. They are unlikely to germinate in the cold climate, but some are washed up every year.

◄ Sea beet is a characteristic plant of shingle beaches. Its seeds are carried by the sea and dumped on the strand line, where they may germinate.

► A short, strong bill that is wedge-shaped and slightly uptilted enables the turnstone to rummage through cast-up debris for the small animals on which it feeds.

visitors such as hedgehogs and, on the Scilly Isles, the white-toothed shrew. On North Ronaldsay in Orkney, the seaweeds on the strand line are the primary food of the local breed of sheep.

Spreading seed

Several coastal plants can be found growing virtually on the strand line. Sea rocket grows closer to the sea than any other flowering land plant, and is one of the first to colonise such habitats. Its long seed pods split open to release small, flattened seeds that lodge in the strand line debris. Yellow horned-poppy and the attractive sea pea are found on some shingle ridges that have been stabilised by strand line

The waves toss a bewildering variety of natural debris on to the strand line, including dead starfish and crabs, empty shells, seaweeds and the egg cases of rays and whelks.

debris, and the beautiful, but rare and declining, oyster plant is found on boulder beaches in the far north and west.

Many of these plants use the sea as an agent of seed dispersal, which is why they are found growing on or near the strand line. The widespread sea sandwort grows just above the strand line where its small white flowers appear in profusion in summer. These are followed by yellowish seed pods that have a shiny, waterproof outer coat that enables them to float. When an extra-high tide reaches the plant the pods are washed away. Many drift far out to sea and perish, but some end up on another shore, cast up on the strand line. Here they may germinate in the debris and grow into new plants.

Many other strand line plants disperse their seeds in this way. The large sea kale, a member of the cabbage family, often grows on shingle

banks. It produces big, white flower heads that are succeeded by small, woody seed pods that spill their seeds into the water. Sea beet, related to beetroot, is also a common find on shingle ridges, and its corky seeds can be carried over great distances.

One of the most exciting finds for a beachcomber is a sea heart, a big flattened seed resembling a large broad bean. It is the seed of *Entada gigas*, a tropical climbing plant from the Caribbean. The seeds fall into the sea and are carried to Britain by the Gulf Stream. It is just one of many big, tropical 'drift seeds' that find their way to British shores, to end up in the heap of tide-washed debris that is the strand line.

WILDLIFE WATCH

When can I find strand line wildlife?

● The best time to visit the beach is in the calm after a storm – but wait until there is no more danger from large waves.

● The progressively smaller tides preceding a neap tide provide the most debris to investigate, as a series of strand lines will form down the shore. The lowest spring tide will expose the most extensive area of shore. Consult the local tide tables and time a visit accordingly.

● A magnifying glass is always useful, and a small knife will help lift encrusting animals from driftwood. Always put them back where you found them.

The Lake District – panoramic views

Few English landscapes can match the grandeur of the Lake District, with its majestic fells and crystal-clear lakes. Winter adds an extra dimension to its beauty, enhanced by the hardy animals that brave the wind and snow.

Glorious in any season, the Lake District is surely at its most spectacular on clear, frosty winter days, when the snowy fells gleam white beneath a cloudless blue sky and the lake waters sparkle in the sunshine.

Winter weather can vary greatly in different areas of the Lake District, which is also known as Lakeland. When the fell tops are shrouded in deep snow, the coastal south may be experiencing much milder days and light rain. The temperature also varies locally. Woodlands are always warmer and more humid than open ground, thanks to the shelter provided by the trees, and while small pools, or tarns, may freeze over, the large lakes usually remain ice-free. In fact, the water of the deeper lakes is not much colder than it is in summer.

The weather changes from day to day, with sudden snow falls followed by rapid thaws, and cold clear days followed by blustery rain. It also varies from year to year, from bitterly cold and snowy to relatively mild and damp. Yet whatever the weather, the incomparable landscape is always a delight, and so is the wildlife.

First impressions might suggest that wildlife abandons the Lake District altogether in winter, but this is not so. It is true that many animals vanish during the colder months,

The sheep that live on the fells of the Lake District are tough upland breeds, such as these Swaledales, able to stay out in all weathers – although they may need extra food.

either because of migration or dormancy. However, others stay on, and are active, throughout the year. They include some surprising residents. The dipper, for example, is a small, rotund, brown and white bird that has the unusual habit of hunting for aquatic insect larvae by swimming and walking underwater in fast-flowing upland streams. This technique is remarkable at any time, but the fact that the bird uses it in winter, except in the very harshest of weather, is little short of amazing.

Many small woodland birds stay through the winter to forage in mixed flocks. Groups of great, blue, marsh, coal and long-tailed tits can often be seen patrolling the woodlands, searching for the invertebrates that spend the season hidden in cracks in bark or rotten wood. These flocks are

sometimes accompanied by nuthatches, which are a relatively recent addition to Lakeland wildlife. They lived in the region in the early 19th century, but had vanished from northern England by 1900. After an absence of half a century they reappeared in the 1950s, but have become well established only in the last 20 years or so.

Northern visitors

Some birds deliberately travel to the Lake District because, for them, its winters are relatively mild. As mainland Europe starts to freeze, flocks of fieldfares and redwings fly south and west, arriving in Lakeland to feed on the berries of rowan, holly and hawthorn. Most move on as the berries are exhausted, but many remain unless the winter is particularly cold, feeding on invertebrates.

Flocks of siskins, redpolls, bramblings, greenfinches and chaffinches also arrive from mainland Europe to feed in Cumbria's woodlands over the winter. These seed-eaters are attracted by the plentiful food, such as beech mast, as well as the milder climate.

Other northern European arrivals head for the lakes, which soon amass flocks of waterfowl. The numbers of goldeneye spending the season on Windermere, for example, may regularly exceed 300. Accompanying them are

▶ The red-brown plumage of the red grouse becomes darker in winter, making it hard to spot among the brown heather high on the fells.

smaller numbers of goosanders, red-breasted mergansers, great-crested grebes and little grebes. This influx of birds to the cold waters of Windermere and other lakes is not as surprising as it might seem, because the larger lakes are full of small fish and invertebrates, and freeze only in the most severe winters, such as the bitter season of 1962–3.

Scarcer winter visitors may include the waxwing, short-eared owl, great grey shrike, snow bunting, smew and bittern. The snow bunting is unusual in that, alone among these birds, it can be found on the high fells during the

▲ During long winter nights, the tawny owl searches for prey, relying heavily on its acute hearing to target small mammals and birds in the dark woods.

▶ A winter visitor from Scandinavia and Iceland, the redwing is lured to the Lake District by its more abundant food, such as tasty berries.

Chaffinches breed widely in the Lake District, and their numbers are swelled by winter migrants moving west from Europe.

coldest part of the season. It joins the relatively few resident species that stay on the fells throughout the winter, including the bird-hunting peregrine. Parts of the Lake District have what is believed to be one of the world's highest densities of inland-breeding peregrines, which leads to intense competition for nest sites. Established pairs therefore try to deter rivals by staying on their territories all winter, as long as they can find sufficient prey. If food runs short, they make for the coast, to hunt among the large flocks of waders and wildfowl to be found there.

The red grouse that live on the heather-clad areas of the fells also prefer to stay on their breeding territories if possible, and the territory-holding adult males are generally last to leave for lower ground when the severe weather hits. However, although it is one of the most characteristic birds of the British uplands, the red grouse is not common in the Lake District because grazing has eliminated much of the heather on which it depends.

Browsing deer

In winter, the snow and wet mud show up mammal tracks well and the lack of leaves on the trees makes the animals more visible. Energy-sapping cold and shortage of food mean that they have to spend more time foraging, often in daylight.

Two native species of deer are common in the Lake District – red deer and roe deer. The much larger red deer is often thought of as a moorland animal, but it also lives in woodland. The herds are active through the winter, but those on the fells move to lower altitudes to escape the worst of the weather and seek better grazing. The rut, or breeding ritual, takes place in autumn, so the hinds are pregnant during winter. This leads to strong competition for grazing, with hinds taking precedence over stags. Since this follows the exertions of the rut, stags often do not get enough food to make good the energy losses that they have sustained. Many die as a

Winter lays a white shroud over the Langdales in the heart of the Lake District, causing small lakes to freeze.

Red deer stags retain their magnificent antlers through the winter, shedding them in spring if they survive the harsh weather and lack of food.

result, and the lifespan of a stag is generally much shorter than that of a hind.

The smaller, more delicate roe deer is a woodland animal. It remains in the woods all the winter, browsing on bramble leaves and the twigs and shoots of trees and shrubs. Both roe and red deer are particularly fond of the leaves of yew trees, and the deer are now so abundant that their winter browsing is preventing the regeneration of yew in many wooded areas of Lakeland.

Opportunist hunters

All the predatory mammals of the Lake District remain active through the winter. Foxes, pine martens, polecats, stoats and weasels feed on whatever they can find, including birds, small mammals and more than the usual amount of carrion.

The otter's existence is made harder because it loses so much energy by swimming in cold water. It needs a lot of fish to compensate, and this dictates where it can live. After almost disappearing from the Lake District altogether during the 1970s it is making a welcome return to some lakes and rivers. It is unlikely to become common in the central Lake District, though, because most of the waters there are naturally low in nutrients and small animals, and therefore do not contain enough fish.

Lying low

Smaller mammals, such as mice and voles, are also awake throughout the winter, feeding on nuts, berries, bulbs, roots and insect larvae, and in turn providing food not only for hunting mammals but also for predatory birds, such as the kestrel and tawny owl.

Several species that are widely thought to hibernate do not actually do so. They simply slow down to avoid the worst of the weather. Badgers, for example, remain underground in really cold weather, conserving energy by remaining relatively inactive, and using up the fat reserves that they accumulated during the autumn. However, they often emerge during spells of milder winter weather to forage for earthworms.

Red squirrels spend wet winter weather in their tree nests, or dreys, but they can be seen moving through the leafless trees on sunny days, and on the ground searching for the nuts and seeds they

The otter is slowly returning to Britain, including to the wilds of the Lake District, where it is most common on the northern lowland rivers.

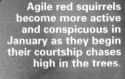

Agile red squirrels become more active and conspicuous in January as they begin their courtship chases high in the trees.

Now recovered from the pesticide poisoning that almost wiped it out in the 1960s and 1970s, the peregrine is thriving in Lakeland.

buried in autumn. Late in the season the approach of spring makes them more active. They chase each other up and down tree trunks, through the tree tops or across the woodland floor. Despite grey squirrels spreading into the area, competing with the reds for food, the woodlands of the Lake District are among the red squirrel's few remaining English strongholds.

Bats, too, can be active in the winter. Although most species sleep until the weather warms up, others don't just hang upside down until spring comes, but occasionally change roost sites or fly out to catch insects. They can sometimes be seen hunting at dusk in mild weather, flitting through the air in pursuit of flies and winter-flying moths.

Hiding away

Some insects and other invertebrates overwinter as eggs, larvae or pupae, while others become dormant. Reptiles and amphibians are also forced into dormancy by the cold weather, and seek secluded places where they are unlikely to be discovered. Toads and common lizards, for example, regularly take refuge inside the dry-stone walls that are common in the Lake District. Some male frogs hibernate at the bottom of their breeding ponds, so they are in place when the females arrive to spawn in the spring.

Whatever their survival strategy, the animals of the Lake District often have to cope with such harsh weather that losses are inevitable. Young animals are particularly vulnerable, and the majority of young that were born or hatched late the previous summer do not survive to see the following spring. Some of the sheep that live half-wild on the fells also fail to survive, despite being some of the hardiest in Britain.

Winter feast

Their bodies do not go to waste, however. Scavengers such as ravens and buzzards do well out of such casualties, and indeed ravens feed mainly on carrion in the winter. Ravens can sometimes be seen

▼ Flooded and half-frozen, this field has attracted some Bewick's swans. Smaller and more goose-like than the familiar mute swan, they are winter visitors from the Arctic tundra.

in large numbers in early winter, and a flock of 30 or 40 of these big, black crows high up in the snowy fells makes an impressive sight.

The importance of carrion to ravens is clear from the way that their life cycle in the Lake District is closely tied to sheep farming. The birds have their young early to take advantage of the extra carrion available at lambing time in the spring, and this means that they must establish their territories and build their nests in the depths of winter. Accordingly, their dramatic aerial displays can often be seen in winter, accompanied by loud, deep, croaking calls that echo across the valleys from fell to fell. They are spectacular symbols of the will to survive in this rugged landscape.

▲ An accomplished scavenger, with a sharp eye for an easy meal, the buzzard is one of the few animals to profit from harsh winter weather.

◄ A snow bunting crouches close to the ground to feed. These birds breed in the Arctic, and so are accustomed to cold weather.

▼ Wildfowl, such as this male goldeneye, congregate on Lake Windermere during the winter, returning to northern continental Europe in spring.

WILDLIFE WATCH

How can I find out more about the Lake District?

Organisations that own or administer regions of the Lake District include:

● Cumbria Wildlife Trust (CWT), which looks after more than 40 nature reserves. For information telephone 01539 816300 or visit www. wildlifetrust.org.uk/cumbria

● The Royal Society for the Protection of Birds (RSPB). Telephone 01767 680551 or visit www.rspb.org.uk

● The National Trust (NT). For the Cumbria Regional Office, telephone 0870 609 5391 or visit www.nationaltrust.org.uk

● English Nature. Telephone 01733 455000 or visit www.english-nature.org.uk

● Forest Enterprise, which is part of the Forestry Commission. For the Cumbria office, telephone 01768 776616 or visit www.forestry.gov.uk

Places to visit in the Lake District

Comprising mountains, streams, lakes and forests, the Lake District National Park attracts many visitors all year round. This map shows some specialist nature reserves, established to conserve particular habitats and their wildlife. Many of these reserves provide information about the habitats, animals and plants of the Lake District as a whole, as well as the other sites managed by that particular organisation.

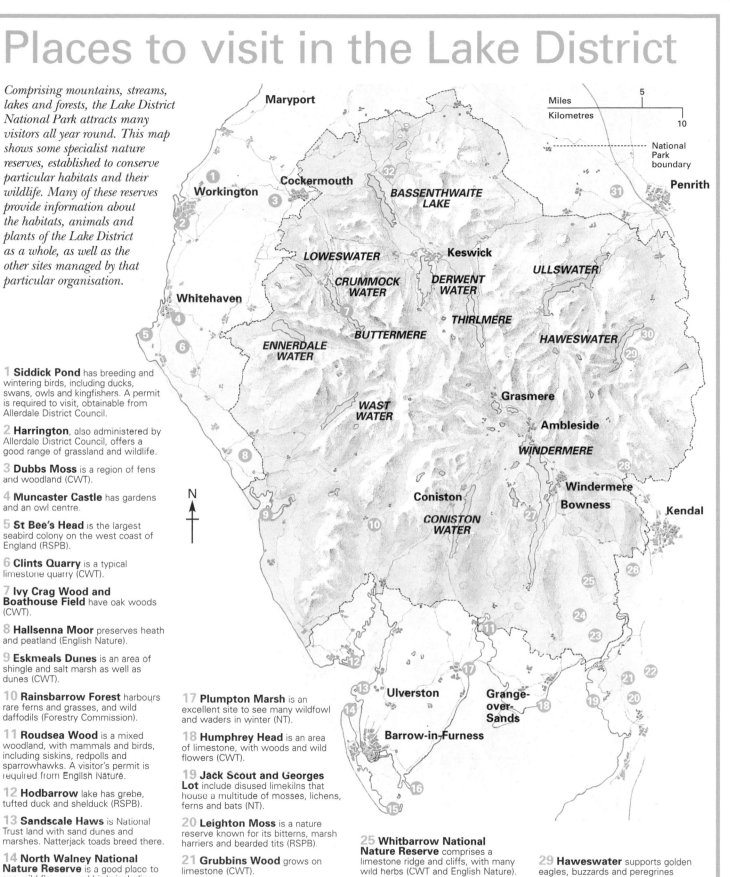

1 Siddick Pond has breeding and wintering birds, including ducks, swans, owls and kingfishers. A permit is required to visit, obtainable from Allerdale District Council.

2 Harrington, also administered by Allerdale District Council, offers a good range of grassland and wildlife.

3 Dubbs Moss is a region of fens and woodland (CWT).

4 Muncaster Castle has gardens and an owl centre.

5 St Bee's Head is the largest seabird colony on the west coast of England (RSPB).

6 Clints Quarry is a typical limestone quarry (CWT).

7 Ivy Crag Wood and Boathouse Field have oak woods (CWT).

8 Hallsenna Moor preserves heath and peatland (English Nature).

9 Eskmeals Dunes is an area of shingle and salt marsh as well as dunes (CWT).

10 Rainsbarrow Forest harbours rare ferns and grasses, and wild daffodils (Forestry Commission).

11 Roudsea Wood is a mixed woodland, with mammals and birds, including siskins, redpolls and sparrowhawks. A visitor's permit is required from English Nature.

12 Hodbarrow lake has grebe, tufted duck and shelduck (RSPB).

13 Sandscale Haws is National Trust land with sand dunes and marshes. Natterjack toads breed there.

14 North Walney National Nature Reserve is a good place to see wild flowers and birds including wildfowl and waders (CWT).

15 South Walney Nature Reserve has a sand and shingle bank and is known for its birdlife, including a breeding colony of gulls (CWT).

16 Foulney Island has shingle banks with wildfowl, waders and seabirds (CWT).

17 Plumpton Marsh is an excellent site to see many wildfowl and waders in winter (NT).

18 Humphrey Head is an area of limestone, with woods and wild flowers (CWT).

19 Jack Scout and Georges Lot include disused limekilns that house a multitude of mosses, lichens, ferns and bats (NT).

20 Leighton Moss is a nature reserve known for its bitterns, marsh harriers and bearded tits (RSPB).

21 Grubbins Wood grows on limestone (CWT).

22 Hale Moss is an area of marsh lying on fine grains of sedimentary rock, called marl (CWT).

23 Meathop Moss consists of raised bogland (CWT).

24 Latterbarrow, an ancient woodland, has butterflies and wild flowers (CWT).

25 Whitbarrow National Nature Reserve comprises a limestone ridge and cliffs, with many wild herbs (CWT and English Nature).

26 Sizergh Castle is a National Trust property. The gardens offer several walks.

27 Ash Landing has butterflies, frogs and lizards (National Trust).

28 Dorothy Farrers Spring Wood is a coppiced wood full of wild flowers and birds (CWT).

29 Haweswater supports golden eagles, buzzards and peregrines (RSPB).

30 Naddle Forest is full of old sessile oaks with red squirrels and woodpeckers (RSPB).

31 Newton Reigny Moss Reserve is an area of fenland (CWT).

32 Thornthwaite Forest has breeding ospreys.

Animals and plants in focus

Waterside watch

- The beaver
- Chinese water deer
- The bittern
- Recognising diving ducks
- The snipe
- Rainbow trout
- The barbel
- The water spider
- Great pond snail

The beaver

Set to live along Britain's river banks once more, the beaver leads a stable family life in and around water. When pairs mate they stay together for life, forming strong bonds with their young.

Until the 12th century, it is likely that beavers lived along many English river banks, and probably Welsh ones too, and they survived until about 1600 in Scotland. Beaver remains are often discovered in archaeological digs, and their former presence is apparent in place names such as Beverley in Yorkshire and Beverley Brook, a tributary of the River Thames.

However, beavers are easy to trap, edible and have useful skins. Under their tails, they have large scent glands that produce a musky substance that was once highly prized for its supposed medicinal value. For these reasons, beavers were ruthlessly hunted for centuries, and became extinct in Britain as well as in many places on the Continent. Apart from some in zoos and wildlife parks and a recent captive trial introduction, beavers are still absent from Britain.

Vegetarian diet

Beavers prefer slow-flowing waters no more than 10m (33ft) wide, bordered by a belt of deciduous trees at least 100m (more than 300ft) wide. They rarely forage more than 60m (200ft) from the water's edge, so they are unlikely to wander around the countryside or raid farmers' crops. Feeding on vegetation, especially grass, herbs and the leaves of water plants, their diet through much of the year consists of more than 300 different plants.

In winter, beavers turn to stripping juicy bark off young trees, especially willow, aspen, poplar and birch. This is useful in some areas because it helps to thin out these common species. By gnawing through young saplings about 50cm (20in) above the ground, beavers fell them to get at higher branches and leaves that are normally out of reach.

RETURN OF THE BEAVER

A trial introduction of six adult beavers at Lower Mill Estate near South Cerney in Gloucestershire took place in 2005. The animals were caught in Bavaria, Germany, and quarantined first. At present, the beavers are confined to a very large enclosure, and cannot be released without a positive impact assessment and a licence from the Department of the Environment, Food and Rural Affairs.

In the late 19th century, several attempts to release beavers into Britain failed. On the Isle of Bute, in 1875, five animals were kept in a large enclosure. Within two years, numbers had increased to 12 and by 1878 there were more than 20. Sadly, by the late 1890s, they had died out. While an attempt to reintroduce them in Suffolk failed, another attempt in Sussex in 1890 fared slightly better – the beavers bred and lived there for 50 years.

By the early 20th century, only very small, isolated populations survived in France, Germany, Norway, Russia, Mongolia and China – in total, about 1200 individuals. From this time to the present, conservationists have reintroduced beavers – so far to at least 50 river systems in 24 European countries. In 1956, for example, beavers were reintroduced successfully to Switzerland. They were brought from southern France and set free near the city of Geneva. In Britain, however, beavers will not be released near to large towns for fear of them being run over on the roads.

Although eating a large amount of tree bark, an adult beaver and its offspring often do so while sitting or floating in the water. This protects them from predators, such as foxes, which might creep up on them on land.

BEAVER FACT FILE

Europe's largest and heaviest rodent, the beaver has dense, waterproof fur for insulation. It uses its broad tail for steering and propelling its torpedo-shaped body through the water. To swim at speed, it moves its tail up and down in time with powerful thrusts of its hind feet.

● **NAMES**
Common name: European beaver
Scientific name: *Castor fiber*

● **HABITAT**
Prefers slow-flowing rivers with adjacent flood plains; also streams and lakes

● **DISTRIBUTION**
Formerly widespread in Britain; reintroduction started in 2005. None in Ireland

● **STATUS**
Extinct but reintroduced successfully to many areas on the Continent; pilot reintroduction scheme at one site in Gloucestershire

● **SIZE**
Length, head and body 75–90cm (30–36in); weight, adult can exceed 30kg (66lb)

● **KEY FEATURES**
Coat yellowish brown to almost black, reddish brown most common; head blunt, legs short, ears and eyes small; tail broad, horizontally flattened and scaly; hind feet webbed, front feet unwebbed with 5 toes

● **HABITS**
Mainly active at night but sometimes in the day, particularly at dusk; always remains in or near water

● **VOICE**
Generally silent but sometimes utters growls, hisses or screams when disturbed or excited; slaps water with tail as warning signal

● **FOOD**
Mainly leaves, grass and bark of plants close to water

● **BREEDING**
At 2–3 years old; 1–6 young, average of 3 per litter, once a year; usually mates in February and the young are usually born in June

● **NEST**
Underground in large burrow

● **YOUNG**
Similar to adult, but smaller; the young remain in the burrow until weaned

● **SIGNS**
Droppings are a dark mass of shredded plant material, especially wood fibres, that soon sink to the bottom of water; large webbed footprints up to 15cm (6in) long; gnawed trees; branches with bark stripped off

Born fully furred and with their eyes open, the young have soft lips and can keep their big teeth out of the way during suckling. The mother lies on her side to make it easier for the young to feed, and weans them at 6–8 weeks.

Distribution map key

■ Present all year round

□ Not present

Long, shiny, brown guard hairs cover soft grey underfur.

For peering above the water surface, the beaver has small eyes near the top of its head.

Flexible toes on the front feet allow the beaver to grip food.

Unique among rodents is the the beaver's large, paddle-like tail.

COYPU – A CAUTIONARY TALE

The reintroduction of the coypu, *Myocastor coypus*, was a disaster in Britain. Coypus are large rodents that, like beavers, live along water margins. They were brought to Britain from South America from 1929 onwards for breeding on fur farms. Some escaped, and others were deliberately released.

Since coypus produce an average of five young per litter, several times per season, numbers built up rapidly, especially as winters were often mild, allowing many animals to survive. The British population increased to about a quarter of a million by the mid-1960s. Coypus undermined river banks, threatening severe flooding. They ate farm crops and destroyed vegetation. In 1981, a campaign to eradicate the copyu was begun and, by late 1989, it was extinct in Britain.

The beaver's front feet are not webbed. Instead, they have supple toes with which the animal can search for food and then manipulate it with delicacy. Although the beaver waddles on land, it can outpace predators by galloping to water.

▲ For about 50 years, copyus lived wild in Britain. They were originally imported by fur farms for their dense, soft, tawny brown fur.

◄ Young coypus are weaned in a few weeks and are themselves able to breed soon afterwards.

To enable them to feed on trees, beavers have special teeth with very strong front enamel. The inner surface is softer and wears down more quickly, creating a sharp cutting edge. Like all rodents, beavers have large incisors that continue to grow as they are worn down.

Burrows, dams and lodges

Beavers spend most of their time in river-bank burrows. They are efficient excavators and usually dig a number of burrows within their territory. A burrow might be just one tunnel or a maze of tunnels, hollowed into the bank from the water and ending in one or more nest chambers. Towards the nest chamber, the burrow rises so that it is about half a metre (1½ft) above water level. Entrance to the burrow is below water level so that it is hidden from predators and not easy for other animals to enter.

Beavers nipping off the stems from the low branches of older trees often has a similar effect to pruning, stimulating more vigorous growth the next spring. They may store whole branches, or gnawed off sections, underwater as a food reserve to eat later in the winter. Beavers rarely eat conifers, and so do no harm to commercial plantations.

▲ In winter, beavers gnaw the bark of trees with their large, yellowish red incisors. A single beaver can fell a 25cm (10in) thick tree in less than four hours, and a family can topple 300 small trees in one winter.

► Beavers sometimes fell small trees and drag them into the water, where they store them to provide food in winter. Cold water temperatures actually help to preserve the nutritional content of bark.

▼ To allow it to see above the surface of the water when swimming, the beaver's eyes are close to the top of its head. Beavers often dive for five or six minutes, but can make dives lasting up to 15 minutes.

In Britain and Europe, beavers build dams and lodges out of fallen trees only where the river bank is not secure enough for a burrow. Unlike their North American relatives, they do not normally build large dams in any case, so are unlikely to alter the flow of rivers and flood farmland.

If beavers build small dams that cause water to back up, this encourages a variety of aquatic waterside plants to grow, benefiting birds and other creatures living in and around the water. Small pools created in fast-flowing upland streams provide feeding and resting places for fish, especially fry. The pools slow the water flow, reducing bank erosion. When there is heavy rainfall, small dams help to prevent flooding and damage to waterside land and property. Pools also act as traps for silt and help to catch the pollutants and surplus fertilisers washed off farmland that would otherwise impact on wildlife in streams and lakes. Beavers also clear unwanted waterside vegetation that blocks the flow of rivers, and which is costly for humans to remove.

Waterside families

Beavers live in small family groups, the young returning to rejoin the family if they can't find a suitable place to set up on their own. Each family has its own territory, with groups spaced along the river bank at intervals of 1–4km (just over ½–2½ miles). In each family, only the oldest female breeds. Beavers do not usually breed until they are three years old and they produce, on average, three young each year. This means that, as they are reintroduced to Britain, numbers are unlikely to escalate out of control.

Once a pair of beavers mate, they are monogamous and stay together until one of them dies. Beavers mate in winter, usually in the water but perhaps in the burrow. The young, or kits, are usually born in early summer and can swim within a few hours, learning in the tunnels. They are too buoyant to dive down the tunnel to the river from the nest chamber, because of their small size and dense fur, until they are about eight weeks old.

During this time, the male patrols the family's territory, scent marking mounds of vegetation and mud dredged from the water, as well tufts of grass, rocks and logs. In water, a beaver spotting an intruder slaps its tail. The loud splash often elicits a response that helps the beaver to decide whether any threat is posed.

If a trespasser arrives among a family group, which usually numbers five or six, beavers may become aggressive towards each other, quivering their tails, lunging and biting.

Reintroduction concerns

One problem to be overcome in reintroducing beavers is a need for stable river banks in which they can burrow. Another is competition with farm animals for food. Over time, the grazing of cattle and sheep prevents the growth of young trees, a vital food source for beavers. Fencing to keep out farm animals would assist beavers and other wildlife, such as kingfishers and water voles, also affected by the trampling of river banks.

A study carried out by Scottish National Heritage suggests that Scotland could support up to 1000 beavers but the Scottish Executive has refused permission for a trial reintroduction. It may be that the first trial reintroduction will be located in Wales, where representatives of the North Wales Wildlife Trust and other conservationists are currently discussing the possibilities with landowners.

Swimming well underwater, a beaver dives to reach its hidden burrow entrance. During a dive, its webbed hind feet and oval, flattened tail propel it forwards while its front feet tuck into its body.

WILDLIFE WATCH

How can I find out more about beavers?

● Visit the Mammal Trust UK's website at www.mtuk.org for news on beavers in Britain. Recently, the Trust has conducted a poll that revealed high public support for the return of the beaver, with 92 per cent of voters in favour of its reintroduction.

● For more information on beavers in Scotland, visit the Scottish Wildlife Trust's website at www.swt.org.uk

● To find out the latest news on beavers in North Wales visit the North Wales Wildlife Trust's website at www.wildlifetrust.org.uk/northwales

Chinese water deer

The rarest deer in Britain, the Chinese water deer is at its most gregarious in winter when it seeks a mate. For the rest of the year, females live in small groups while males lead a mainly solitary life.

Chinese water deer were introduced to London Zoo from China before being transferred, in 1896, to Woburn Park in Bedfordshire. Boosted by more imports, they bred so successfully that soon there were more than a hundred of them and in 1929 some were transferred to what is now Whipsnade Wild Animal Park where they thrived. Many escaped into the surrounding countryside, and their numbers have gradually increased.

In the 1950s, Chinese water deer were released on the Cambridgeshire fenlands, near Woodwalton, and 100–200 animals now live there. Others escaped from zoos and wildlife collections around the country to form herds. Not all survived – those in Northamptonshire, Shropshire and Hampshire, for example, have now died out. By the early 1990s, several hundred water deer roamed the Norfolk Broads, with more often seen in other parts of East Anglia. Within 100 years, the total wild population has probably risen to nearly 2000 animals.

Living near water

The Chinese water deer and the muntjac deer were introduced to Britain at the same time and place, but water deer have spread much more slowly. This is partly because the muntjac was subsequently released at many more sites, but also because water deer favour damp areas, particularly reedbeds and wet woodlands. There are not many of these in Britain, and they are spaced out so that the deer cannot travel easily from one region to another. However, they do spill over on to arable farmland, especially fields of wheat, carrots and beans. Land left fallow by farmers has benefited water deer because they can feed and hide among the weeds.

MOULTING

In autumn, the Chinese water deer grows its pale grey-brown or plain sandy brown winter fur. Rather stiff and bristly, the fur consists of hollow brittle hairs that break easily, leaving patches and what look like scars. The deer moult back to their summer coat in April or May, when they sometimes appear tatty and rather moth-eaten. In summer, the coat is short and russet coloured, and makes the deer look sleek in comparison to its stocky winter appearance. The deer's legs appear slender and its ears seem large and prominent.

When the ground is covered in snow, the Chinese water deer is forced to search for food, in particular brambles, during the day more often than at other times. Usually, it is most active at dawn and dusk.

CHINESE WATER DEER FACT FILE

Small, shy creatures, Chinese water deer are often mistaken for the diminutive muntjac. In fact, adults are in between the muntjac and the roe deer in size. With hind legs that are longer than their forelegs, water deer have rumps that rise above shoulder height.

● **NAMES**
Common names: Chinese water deer, barking deer
Scientific name: *Hydropotes inermis*

● **HABITAT**
Reedbeds, wet woodland and arable farmland

● **DISTRIBUTION**
Mainly parts of East Anglia, also Bedfordshire, Hertfordshire, Berkshire and Cambridgeshire

● **STATUS**
Rare, but population probably increasing slowly

● **SIZE**
Length 90–95cm (36–37½in); height at shoulder 50–60cm (20–24in); weight, adult 11–19kg (24–42lb)

● **KEY FEATURES**
Pale sandy brown or grey-brown coat in winter, reddish brown in summer; large ears; males have no antlers but tusk-like canine teeth

● **HABITS**
Particularly active in early morning and evening, but also feed during daytime

● **VOICE**
Growling bark when alarmed; loud squeaks and whistles

● **FOOD**
Mostly grasses, sedges and rushes; wild flowers and brambles; occasionally farm crops

● **BREEDING**
Rut November–December, sometimes into January; 1–4 fawns (usually 2 or 3) born May–July

● **YOUNG**
Darker than adult, white spots on coat disappear after about 8 weeks; weaned at 3 months

● **SIGNS**
Pellets 1–1.5cm (½–⅝in) long; tiny cloven hooves leave slotted footprints 4cm (1½in) long; tufts of fur scattered during moult

Distribution map key

■ Present all year round

□ Not present

▲ Like domestic cattle, Chinese water deer are ruminants, which means that a period of grazing is followed by a period of rest. While lying concealed among long grass and vegetation, the deer regurgitate food to be chewed and swallowed again.

▶ Black droppings are deposited singly in piles that can number from two or three to a hundred or more.

Haunch, or rump, is higher than the shoulder and has no white patch, distinguishing it from muntjac and roe deer.

Variable in colour, the thick winter coat is often pale brown.

Large, rounded ears are very furry inside.

The male has distinctive, long, tusk-like canine teeth.

BATTLE SCARS

The Chinese water deer is the only wild deer in Britain in which neither sex has antlers. Instead, the bucks have prominent tusks. These are canine teeth, which grow for the first 18 months of life to a length of about 7cm (2¾in). They are razor sharp along their rear edge due to being rubbed continuously against the lower jaw.

If a buck is cornered in a fight with another male, it uses its tusks in slashing and stabbing actions that can inflict serious wounds on its opponent. Many bucks show the scars from such conflicts. Older bucks often have very tattered ears as a reminder of their many battles. Eye damage may lead to blindness, but fights rarely result in death.

Normally such thin, pointed teeth would be in danger of snapping off if treated roughly. However, the tusks are embedded in fibrous material in the gum, which allows them to be deflected rather than broken. They can also be moved by muscular action, so the buck can keep them out of the way during feeding. Does do not have tusks but do have small canine teeth, not normally present in deer.

Confrontations with a rival, particularly during the mating season, may result in violence, so many bucks have scars. The older the animal, the more battle-scarred it is likely to be.

Water deer escape detection easily amid the thick cover provided by reedbeds and wet woodlands. These timid animals are always on the alert, with excellent hearing to warn them of any potential threat.

Chinese water deer eat mainly grasses, sedges and rushes, while about a quarter of their diet consists of leaves of various wild flowers. Water deer hiding in wooded areas eat more leaves, bark and twigs, nipped off shrubs and low tree branches, than those living mainly on grassy slopes or open farmland. Where the water deer lives in its favourite wet, woody areas, there may be up to 20 per square kilometre (50 per square mile), but on farmland and other areas, where there is less food, numbers tend to be lower.

Each Chinese water deer has a territory of around 5–25 hectares (12–62 acres). Older males, or bucks, often occupy a much smaller patch than females, or does, and some bucks defend

a personal territory of just two hectares (five acres). Some bucks do not defend a territory at all, preferring to wander freely. Does are rarely territorial, but will defend their own area during breeding. At other times, does gather together in loose groups, but these rarely comprise more than about five animals. If alarmed, the deer run away in different directions.

Aggressive bucks

Most sightings of water deer are of single animals. Male water deer, in particular, are solitary and unsociable. If two bucks do meet, their behaviour is often aggressive. They use their teeth to make a slightly mechanical, clicking sound. The animals approach on stiff legs and look each other warily up and down.

They might then start 'parallel walking', strutting along 10–20m (33–66ft) apart, in the same direction, each trying to determine whether or not the other is going to give way. One buck might back down at this stage and allow himself to be chased off. If not, a fight will break out. The bucks prance about, each trying to sink its tusks into its opponent. One or both animals may retire with deep cuts around the neck and flanks. More evidence of a recent fight is provided by the tufts of fur that lie on the ground afterwards.

Courtship behaviour

The Chinese water deer's mating season – or rut – occurs from late autumn and into winter, usually in November and December, with some animals mating in January. During this time the bucks follow does closely, with their necks outstretched and heads held low. They make rotating movements with their heads, which result in a sound of slapping ears. Scent is an important part of courtship, and the bucks sniff the air to determine when the does are ready to mate, frequently making plaintive birdlike whistles or squeaking noises. Does wander without constraint, crossing the territories of several bucks. Each buck pays attention to any doe that has entered its domain. Some circle

Once a Chinese water deer finds a place to drink, it returns regularly. The deer tend to use the same paths and tracks to reach their favoured feeding and drinking spots or to return to protective cover.

◄ Fawns are mostly born out in the open in long grass, or in light cover. They weigh 0.6–1kg (1⅓–2lb) and are able to stand and walk within an hour of being born.

▼ The Chinese water deer is the only British deer that regularly produces twins and triplets. The fawns are nourished by their mother's milk for up to three months, but also begin eating grass from an early age.

females in an attempt to keep them from moving on. Bucks may mate with more than one doe.

Female water deer can breed when they are a year old, but usually do not do so until their second year. Young bucks may try to hold a territory, but will probably not achieve many matings until they are two years old.

Hidden fawns

Female water deer produce more young than any other deer – usually twins or triplets but sometimes as many as four fawns. These are born in May or June and sometimes July, following a pregnancy that lasts around six or seven months. For the first two months of life, the fawns have dark brown coats that are flecked with white spots. This patterned coat helps to break up their outlines and makes the fawns difficult to see, especially among long grass or sun-dappled undergrowth.

The mother hides each fawn separately to reduce the risk of a predator, such as a fox and, occasionally, a stoat or crow, finding and killing them all. Visiting the offspring several times a day, the mother grooms and feeds them. After each visit, the fawns may move to another hiding place, making it difficult for their mother to find them again. Searching for her offspring, the mother might make a sound like a gentle whistle in likely areas. Occasionally, two or three fawns are found together. After the first month, fawns spend less time lying in their hiding places. They also start to select more exposed sites, such as in short grass.

The fawns grow rapidly, putting on about 100g (3½oz) per day. As time goes by they suckle less and by three months they are weaned. They are able to nibble grass and other vegetation from a few

WILDLIFE WATCH

Where can I see Chinese water deer?

● The best place to see water deer is at Whipsnade Wild Animal Park in Bedfordshire, where about 400 to 600 deer roam free on the hillsides and among the zoo animal enclosures.

● There are also around 250 Chinese water deer living free in Woburn Park, Bedfordshire. Here they can be easily seen from the roads and picnic sites.

● Chinese water deer may also be spotted occasionally among reedbeds in the Norfolk Broads and at Cley on the Norfolk coast.

days old. Larger fawns may socialise with others that are not their siblings. They remain vulnerable, however. Up to 40 per cent of newborns die within the first month of life, usually due to exposure to cold and wet weather. By the time winter arrives, well over half the young may have died, either through the weather or being taken by predators. Flooding or a long period when the ground is covered in snow may increase the mortality rate. Adult water deer have no predators in Britain except humans, and occasionally dogs, but the deer are able to smell humans from 100m (over 300ft) away, so they are usually able to hide in good time.

An area may not have sufficient food for resident water deer and the young that have survived. In this case, some of the young will be driven away to find another place to live. Such animals may need to cross roads or even inland waters – the deer are strong swimmers. This finding of new territories causes no problems because water deer are not a nuisance in the countryside. Confined to areas where conditions suit them, they inflict little damage on farm crops and young forest trees.

▼ This fawn has replaced its brown baby fur with a russet adult summer coat. During daytime, water deer spend about half of their time grazing, hidden among tall grasses and reeds.

The bittern

A lone male bittern's unmistakable song – known as 'booming' – travels over lowland swamps and marshes as it warns away rivals and calls for a mate.

Most of the bittern's time is spent hidden among waterside plants. It particularly favours places where the common reed, *Phragmites*, is abundant. Reedbeds where reeds of different ages are interspersed with channels and areas of deeper water are ideal because they provide a variety of different conditions for nesting and feeding. While the bittern may emerge to feed in the open, it is seldom seen far from cover into which it will disappear quickly if disturbed.

In winter, even those bitterns that move away from their breeding grounds continue to seek reedbeds. Only the harshest winter can force the birds away from that environment. Bitterns have been spotted in unlikely places –

including town centres – in freezing weather conditions. Such birds have been driven so far from their natural home by sheer desperation to find food and many may not survive.

Courtship booming

Many birds engage in visual courtship displays but the bittern lives a solitary life, mostly hidden among the reeds of its waterside home, so a visual display would be ineffective. Instead, from late January through to April or even June, the male booms from a regular calling place within its territory, advertising his presence to rival males and potential mates. One way to describe the song of the male bittern is to liken it to the sound produced by blowing across the top of a glass bottle.

UNIQUE BOOMS

Recent research has shown that, by slowing down a recording of a bittern's boom, small differences can be detected between individual calls. No two birds' booms are alike. This has enabled researchers to tell apart the territories and movements of individual bitterns. It seems likely that the louder booms, which carry a long way, are uttered by older, stronger males. Even those booms from younger males that do not seem loud resonate powerfully across vast expanses of marshland and fens.

In the clear air of such places, the boom of a male bittern can travel up to 5km (3 miles). The male booms at any time of day, but especially at dawn and dusk, and it is likely that bitterns can recognise the subtle differences in the calls of different males. This enables them to distinguish one individual from another – and females may be able to discern the age and vigour of the calling male.

In winter, the bittern may venture into the open in search of food, and will eat small mammals and birds when fish, frogs and insects are in short supply.

BITTERN FACT FILE

Smaller than its familiar relative, the grey heron, the bittern is much larger than the crakes and rails with which it shares its reedbed home. In winter, British bitterns are joined by birds from Europe and the swell in numbers means they may be seen in open marshy areas.

● **NAMES**
Common names: bittern, great bittern, Eurasian bittern
Scientific name: *Botaurus stellaris*

● **HABITAT**
Dense reedbeds, sometimes emerges to feed in more open areas; smaller reedbeds and other open marshy areas in winter

● **DISTRIBUTION**
In summer, breeding restricted mainly to nature reserves in East Anglia and Lancashire; more widespread in winter, especially in south-eastern England

● **STATUS**
Rare, numbers increasing slowly although fluctuations occur; 55 booming males recorded in 2004, 46 in 2005; usually fewer than 100 winter visitors from continental Europe

● **SIZE**
Length 70–80cm (28–32in); weight 0.9–1.1kg (2–2½lb)

● **KEY FEATURES**
Mottled golden brown, reddish brown, black and buff plumage, with black crown and moustache; broad, rounded wings; long, mobile neck; sharp bill

● **HABITS**
Secretive; particularly active at dawn and dusk; often flies between feeding areas

● **VOICE**
Booming song of male heard in late winter and spring; both male and female use a harsh '*aark, aark*' call

● **FOOD**
Mainly fish, especially eels, frogs, toads, newts and large insects, as well as worms, crustaceans, spiders, lizards, small mammals and birds

● **BREEDING**
Males establish territories and begin booming from late January; eggs laid April–May; young birds leave home reedbed August–September

● **NEST**
Consists of mound of reeds and other plants sited above water level in dense reedbeds

● **EGGS**
4–6 olive brown eggs, incubated by female, hatch after about 25 days

● **YOUNG**
Cared for by female; leave nest after 2–3 weeks but fed by female until they fledge at about 7–8 weeks

After two to three weeks, the young may stray away from the nest, clambering through the closely packed, tall reeds. They first adopt the typical head-up alarm posture at about eight days old.

Distribution map key

■ Present all year round

■ Present during winter months

□ Not present

A black crown and moustache mark the head.

On the upperparts, the plumage is golden brown, mottled and barred with black.

Dagger-like, the bill is greenish yellow.

The feathers on the throat are thick and elongated.

Yellow buff, striped with reddish brown, the underparts are also barred and spotted with black.

The bittern is fully protected under Schedule 1 of the Wildlife and Countryside Act, 1981. Special penalties are incurred by anyone caught interfering with the birds or disturbing their nests or young.

Stealthy hunter

A hunting bittern stalks its prey patiently. If observed, it appears to move in slow motion until the last moment. Wading in shallow water, the bird often pauses and stands motionless for long periods, all the while scanning its surroundings.

Treading slowly to avoid alarming its prey, the bittern edges closer towards it.

With its head retracted, the bittern makes a slight movement from side to side, which helps it to judge where its target is travelling.

Leaving home

Once a courting male has mated with a female, the female builds a nest in the reedbed. This is a platform made of reeds and other water plants, lined with finer plant material.

The female lays four, five or six olive brown eggs in April or May. While she incubates the eggs, the male may mate with one or more other females – some males have two or three mates a year, and possibly as many as five. The young hatch after 25 days and the female feeds them for the next seven weeks or so. Males that have only one mate may bring food to the nest, but most males take very little part in rearing their offspring.

Soon after the young can fly (at around two months old), they leave their home territories and travel to different reedbeds for the autumn. By mid-winter, they are joined by bitterns that have migrated to Britain from northern and eastern Europe. As the winter population grows, bitterns may be seen in smaller reedbeds and other marshy places. During harsh weather, bittern mortality reaches its peak. Survivors return to their traditional, larger reedbeds in late winter. They are able to breed at one year old, and may live for 10 years or more.

Special characteristics

Particular features equip the bittern well for living in reedbeds. Its plumage markings mimic the colours and patterns of its reedy surroundings so that the bittern is well camouflaged as it hunts. With its long, sharp bill, it can either seize or stab its prey. Although the bittern feeds mainly on fish, it may also eat insects, worms and amphibians, and even small mammals and birds. The bittern must catch enough prey for its substantial size, so much of its time is spent foraging.

▲ As it wades through shallow margins in search of prey, the bittern snakes its way through the reeds. A bird may rake its feet along the bed to flush out prey, stabbing it quickly with its bill.

▶ The bittern has a remarkable ability to change shape. When the weather is cold, the bird withdraws its neck and fluffs out its feathers. The resulting egg-shape looks nothing like its sleek hunting profile.

Amazingly agile, the bittern's long toes spread the bird's weight as it walks across floating marshland plants. It is also adept at climbing tall reeds by grasping several stems at once with its toes. Like other members of the heron family, the bittern has comb-like serrations on the claws of the middle toe of each foot. These are used for grooming and are well suited for combing fish scales and slime out of feathers.

With one swift movement, the bittern extends its neck to snatch up a young eel in its dagger-like bill, or even spear it on the tip.

The bittern shakes the prey thoroughly and bites it many times before swallowing it head first.

BITTERN CALENDAR

FEBRUARY • MARCH

Bitterns leave smaller marshes and reedbeds and return to their breeding territories. From February, males are booming regularly to establish territories and attract females.

APRIL • MAY

Males continue to boom as the birds build nests. In April, females start to lay their eggs, which hatch about a month later. Females may be seen in flight as they bring back food for their young.

JUNE • JULY

After two to three weeks, the young birds venture a short distance from the nest and are fed on ever-larger prey. A month later, they are able to fly and some disperse in July.

AUGUST • SEPTEMBER

Young bitterns leave their home territories, moving to other reedbeds and marshes for the winter. Adults may remain on breeding grounds for the whole winter or until the first frosts.

OCTOBER • NOVEMBER

Continental bitterns, escaping from cold European weather, arrive in southern and eastern Britain. These birds may be found in small reedbeds, old gravel workings and riverside marshes.

DECEMBER • JANUARY

During freezing weather, bitterns may be driven out of their reedbeds temporarily to search for food beside areas of open water. At such times, they may be seen in unusual places.

Bittern stance

When disturbed, the bittern often adopts a distinctive posture, called the bittern stance, with its neck and body fully stretched upwards and its bill pointing to the sky. Its plumage markings now camouflage it even more effectively than usual in the reedbed.

A bittern on its nest senses danger. It crouches with its wings outspread and bill raised, ruffling up all its body feathers. Swaying slightly in imitation of reeds as they move in the breeze, the bittern stays in this pose until the perceived danger is past.

The bittern's eyes are the only parts of it to move, swivelling around to keep track of the intruder's movements. If provoked, the bird may attack.

Most birds secrete preen oil from a gland at the base of their tails, spreading this on to their plumage with their bills before preening. By contrast, the bittern, and other birds of the heron family, produce powder down – a talcum-powder-like substance – rather than preen oil. Powder down comes from special feathers, which grow in several pairs of tracts on the breast and rump. These break up to form a highly absorbent, fine blue powder. The bittern picks up the powder in its bill and applies it to its soiled feathers, where it soaks up fish and eel slime, scales and other dirt. After a recent application, the bird looks as if it has been dusted in blue flour. The colour can vary through different shades of blue to purple. It fades between applications and may be washed off by rain.

◄ **The fluffy, ginger youngsters hatch one after another in the space of a week. They are incubated continuously when small and fed by the female, mainly on regurgitated tadpoles.**

▼ **With roving orange eyes, the bittern watches whatever startled it. The bird may stay in this stance for up to 45 minutes, blending in with its background, until it can be certain that there is no danger.**

Bitterns tend to spend more time on the ground than in flight and if a bird is flushed from cover it will usually travel just a short distance before dropping back into the reeds. Its wings are broad and round-ended and it flies with its head and neck pulled back rather than stretched out, swooping low over the reed tops. Bitterns are at their most active at dusk.

Fluctuating population

Before 1840, the bittern was a familiar sight in Britain and Ireland. In fenland areas, it was even hunted and eaten roasted. By the 19th century, hunting was partly responsible for the decline in bittern numbers. Trophy hunters and egg collectors took their toll on the remaining population. The last eggs were collected in 1868 and the last young birds were seen in 1886. It was then assumed that the bittern was extinct as a breeding bird in the British Isles, although migrant birds were still seen in winter.

There was no further sign of breeding bitterns until 1911, when chicks were spotted on the Norfolk Broads – migrant birds from colder parts of Europe had chosen to stay on to breed. Over the next few decades the bittern population slowly increased, mainly in East Anglia but bitterns also moved into Lancashire and Kent, and then Scotland, Wales and Ireland. By 1954, there were 80 booming

---

DID YOU KNOW?

Old country names for the bittern include bitter-bump, bog blutter, bull of the bog, bog-bumper and butter bump.

Male bitterns are highly aggressive in the defence of their territories and birds have been found with mortal stab wounds. They will also engage in aerial combat, circling and lunging at each other, using their sharp bills as weapons.

males in the British Isles. However, this was a peak after which numbers declined. By 1997 there were only 11 or 12 left. Since then, the work of conservationists, helped by enlightened landowners and funding from the European Union (EU), is restoring the bittern population gradually. It is hoped that by 2020 at least 100 booming males will be recorded.

Ongoing research is hampered by the bittern's secretive nature and preference for thick reedbeds. Most recently, young birds have been fitted with tiny radio transmitters, allowing them to be tracked as they move from place to place.

Loss of reedbeds

There is much speculation about what caused the 20th-century decline in the bittern population, but land drainage is likely to be the chief problem. Today, most bitterns nest on nature reserves because elsewhere mostly just tiny remnants of reedbeds have been left by the drainage of fens and marshes. Small patches of reed can provide a winter home for a bittern, but they are of little use to a nesting bird because they do not provide sufficient cover or food for growing youngsters. In the Norfolk Broads, disturbance caused by holiday-makers has also resulted in bitterns being disinclined to breed there.

The loss of large reedbeds is not the whole story, however. In the 1950s, at the start of the most recent decline, pesticides had an adverse impact on many birds. Raptors and other birds near the top of the food chain, such as herons, suffered the most evident decline, and bitterns must also have been affected. Other agricultural chemicals may not pollute the water directly, but they can cause blooms of algae to develop. Algae in water causes a reduction in numbers of fish and waterside insects.

Reedbeds are no longer managed as they were in the past, and this is also likely to have contributed to the bittern's decline. When reedbeds were regularly cut for thatching, there was a patchwork of reeds of different ages. This suited bitterns much better than neglected reedbeds. Reeds of different heights allow areas of clear water while still providing the birds with enough cover for nesting and roosting. Reedbeds on RSPB and other reserves are now specially managed to provide just the right mix of new and old growth. As a result, bittern numbers have remained stable.

The current bittern population is too small to be secure, and one or two harsh winters could result in the bittern disappearing from Britain once again. To guard against this, the RSPB is creating new reedbeds in such places as the RSPB reserves at Lakenheath Fen in Suffolk, Needingworh Quarry and Ouse Fen in Cambridgeshire, Dungeness in Kent and Ham Wall Reserve, near Ashcott in the Avalon Marshes in Somerset. These not only provide suitable breeding conditions for bitterns, but also encourage a variety of other wildlife that has diminished in recent years. Small numbers of bitterns are already feeding and nesting at these restored reedbeds.

In flight the bittern resembles a large owl, with the exception of the head and bill. However, these distinguishing features are difficult to see from behind or in poor light.

WILDLIFE WATCH

Where can I see bitterns?

● A winter viewing scheme has recently been set up in the Lee Valley Country Park near Waltham Abbey in north London. There are three hides at the Fisher's Green watchpoint, including one called the Bittern Hide overlooking a part of the reedbed where the birds are often seen. To contact the Lee Valley Information Centre, telephone 01992 702200 or visit www.leevalleypark.org.uk To contact the RSPB, telephone 01295 676445 or visit www.rspb.org.uk.

● Near the Lee Valley, the RSPB reserve of Rye Meads has wintering bitterns. To contact them, telephone 01992 708383.

● The RSPB reserves at Leighton Moss, in Lancashire, and Minsmere, in Suffolk, have breeding bitterns. The birds may be seen at almost any time of year. To contact Leighton Moss, telephone 01524 701601. To contact Minsmere, telephone 01728 648281.

● The National Trust reserve at Wicken Fen in Cambridgeshire is a superb site for viewing bitterns. To contact them, telephone 01353 720274.

● Bitterns should be viewed only on nature reserves that offer public viewing. The birds should not be disturbed, especially when nesting or feeding in harsh weather.

Recognising diving ducks

Distinguished from other wildfowl by their habit of frequently disappearing below the water's surface when feeding, diving ducks are attractive visitors to shallow coastal waters and lakes.

Every winter, lakes, estuaries and coastal waters in Britain and Ireland attract thousands of diving ducks from their breeding grounds in the far north. Most of these tough, eye-catching birds can be seen only in winter, even though small numbers breed in the British Isles. The breeding population of the common scoter, for example, consists of just 200 or so pairs that nest in the remote north and west of Scotland and Ireland. In winter its numbers are swelled to more than 40,000 birds, living around British coasts. Most of the other diving ducks follow a similar pattern. Some, such as the eider, goldeneye, goosander and red-breasted merganser, breed in Britain in variable numbers – mainly in the north and west – but the majority are either scarce or absent during the warmer months. The absentees breed mainly in northern Europe and Asia, and many are Arctic nesters. The only species that is really widespread in Britain in summer is the tufted duck, but even this is far more common in winter.

Diving for food

The term 'diving duck' does not refer to any one group or genus of ducks in particular, but encompasses a variety of species that obtain their food by diving well below the surface of the water. This distinguishes them from dabbling ducks, such as the mallard, that normally feed at the surface or by up-ending. Diving ducks are capable of relatively long, deep dives, and need little time at the surface to catch their breath.

The chestnut-headed male pochard is a handsome bird that usually is seen feeding in the shallows of well-vegetated lake margins. It often gathers in large single-sex flocks.

WILDLIFE WATCH

When and where can I find diving ducks?

● The months from October to March are by far the best times to look for diving ducks. Many form flocks on inland lakes and reservoirs as well as around coasts, and they are easy to watch with the aid of binoculars, and preferably a telescope. Relatively few diving ducks remain in the British Isles all year round.

● Good numbers of tufted ducks and far fewer pochards breed in Britain, but both become more numerous and widespread in winter on freshwaters, thanks to an influx of migrant birds from mainland Europe. During severe weather, in particular, they are often joined by smaller numbers

of goldeneyes and scaups, but the latter are scarce inland, occurring mainly on sheltered coastal waters.

● Eiders are most common around the coasts of Scotland and northern England where they are present throughout the year, although small numbers winter farther south.

● The common scoter is a rare breeding bird in Britain, but winter visitors from farther afield mean that it is quite common as a non-breeding visitor. It forms large flocks on the sea, especially off sandy coasts, and is often seen in company with smaller numbers of velvet scoters.

● Long-tailed ducks are exclusively winter visitors to Britain from their Arctic breeding grounds. Large flocks can be found in many bays around the Scottish coast – the birds favour extremely rough water, often just where the waves begin to break on shallow-shelving beaches. Smaller numbers turn up farther south – some on inland lakes during and after severe winter gales or prolonged cold spells.

● Goosanders and red-breasted mergansers breed beside fast-flowing upland rivers in the north and west of Britain. Outside the summer breeding season, mergansers favour

sheltered rocky coasts and estuaries where fish are abundant. Goosanders, by contrast, prefer large, fish-stocked lakes and reservoirs, mainly in the north of the region.

● Smews are unpredictable visitors that appear in small numbers each winter. Their arrival is always associated with severe winter weather on the Continent.

● Look for ruddy ducks on well-vegetated lakes and gravel pits, mainly in central and southern Britain. Small numbers breed at scattered sites in north Wales, northern England, southern Scotland and Northern Ireland.

Since they are used to the rigours of northern climates, diving ducks are not easily discouraged by bad weather. They appear to be indifferent to any extremes the British climate can produce. Some diving ducks form large winter flocks that roost and feed on the water. They mainly favour the company of their own kind, but where feeding conditions are good they may gather in mixed flocks, especially on fresh water, providing a spectacle that can brighten up the dullest winter days.

Lakes and seas
Wintering diving ducks fall into two main categories, according to their preference for shallow seas and estuaries, or lakes, flooded gravel pits and reservoirs. The eider, for example, is a sea duck, while the pochard favours lakes. However, there is considerable overlap, particularly during severe weather when some sea ducks may move inland to

feed on large, ice-free lakes and other waters, alongside freshwater species.

Diving ducks' diet reflects their choice of habitat, as well as the feeding adaptations of some species. Members of the genus *Aythya* – the tufted duck, pochard and scaup – eat molluscs, insects and

Goosanders begin to establish breeding pairs while they are still in winter flocks. Here a brown-headed female responds to a male's advances by raising her crest and lowering her head.

crustaceans, as well as plant material, although the proportions vary from species to species and according to availability. Some of the sea ducks – the eider, common scoter, velvet scoter, long-tailed duck and goldeneye – feed on marine molluscs and crustaceans. The eider, in particular, feeds almost exclusively on mussels. A further group of ducks known as sawbills – the goosander, red-breasted merganser and smew – feed mainly on fish in winter, and their bills are

equipped with serrated edges that enable them to catch and hold their slippery prey.

Exotic escape
The only other diving duck likely to be seen is the ruddy duck, which is a native of North America. Some escaped from captivity at the Wildfowl and Wetland Trust's reserve at Slimbridge in Gloucestershire in the late 1950s, and the species has been breeding in the wild since at least 1960. Ruddy ducks live on shallow, plant-fringed lakes and gravel pits, and dive in search of small animals and seeds to eat.

▼ **The female eider is duller than the male. Both sexes have triangular tracts of feathers on long, wedge-shaped bills.**

EASY GUIDE TO SPOTTING DIVING DUCKS

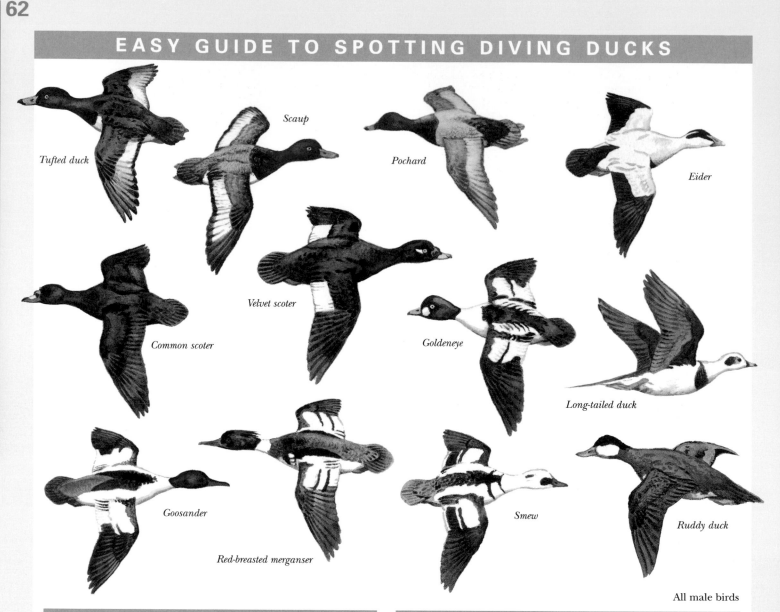

Tufted duck

Scaup

Pochard

Eider

Common scoter

Velvet scoter

Goldeneye

Long-tailed duck

Goosander

Red-breasted merganser

Smew

Ruddy duck

All male birds

WHAT ARE DIVING DUCKS?

● Like all other wildfowl, diving ducks belong to the family Anatidae, a group that displays considerable diversity in size, appearance and lifestyle.

● The pochard, tufted duck and scaup belong to the genus *Aythya.* They are medium-sized ducks with broad, flattened bills.

● The eider, in the genus *Somateria,* is a large and bulky bird with a long, powerful, wedge-shaped bill, which it uses for tearing mussels from rocks. The eider is a completely marine species.

● Common and velvet scoters, members of the the genus *Melanitta,* have powerful bills. Both species breed beside fresh water but spend the winter by the sea.

● The goldeneye – in the genus *Bucephala* – is a conspicuously marked bird with a small bill and large head. In winter it can be found by the coast and on large inland lakes.

● The long-tailed duck belongs to the genus *Clangula.* Its plumage is very variable according to sex and season, and the males have long tails for most of the year.

● The goosander, red-breasted merganser and smew are called sawbills on account of their narrow, serrated bills, which they use for catching fish. They belong to the genus *Mergus.*

● The ruddy duck is a so-called 'stifftail' duck. An introduced species, it belongs to the genus *Oxyura.*

Distribution map key

■ Present all year round	■ Present during winter months
■ Present during breeding season	□ Not present

HOW CAN I IDENTIFY DIVING DUCKS?

● The male tufted duck and scaup are similar. Look for the former's tufted head and the latter's pale grey (not black) back. Females of both species are mainly brown, but a scaup has more white on the face.

● Male pochards are recognised by their rusty red heads. Females usually show a pale 'spectacle' around the eye.

● Eider plumage varies according to age and season. The distinctive bill is common to both sexes.

● Scoters are dark plumaged, although male velvet scoters have white on the wing and around the eye. Female common scoters have pale cheeks, while female velvets have pale spots on the head.

● Goldeneye have bulbous-looking heads – the female's is chocolate brown while the male's is green-glossed black.

● A long-tailed duck has an elongated look with much white on the body and unmarked dark wings.

● The goosander and red-breasted merganser both have relatively long, narrow, slightly hook-tipped bills. The smew has a short, slightly broader bill.

● A ruddy duck is recognised by its small size and long tail, which is often cocked at an angle.

A goldeneye performs a characteristic jump-dive. These ducks can remain underwater for 20 seconds or more.

TUFTED DUCK *Aythya fuligula*

The male tufted duck is one of the most distinctive small ducks, with striking pied plumage, a prominent black crest, a golden eye and a pale bluish grey bill with a black tip. The female is mostly brown with paler barred brown flanks and belly, and similar bill and eye colours to the male, but only a short tuft on her head. In flight, both sexes show a broad white wingbar. Large flocks of tufted ducks gather on open water. Like scaup, tufted ducks dive frequently and for long periods.

- **SIZE**
  40–47cm (16–18½in)

- **NEST**
  A hollow near water, hidden by vegetation

- **BREEDING**
  Lays 8–11 greenish grey eggs in March–May

- **FOOD**
  Aquatic molluscs, crustaceans and insects, plus some plant matter

- **HABITAT**
  Large bodies of open water, including wide rivers

- **VOICE**
  Male usually silent; female gives harsh, low *'karr karr'* call, especially in flight

- **DISTRIBUTION**
  Widespread; increasing in areas where new reservoirs and gravel pits are created

Although the long tuft on the male's head may be conspicuous, it can also be flattened to create a more rounded outline.

Black-and-white plumage

Short tuft

May have white mark at base of bill

Female

Male

SCAUP *Aythya marila*

A male scaup bears some resemblance to a male tufted duck, but the head is dark glossy green rather than dark purplish, there is no tuft and the back is whitish with a delicate grey wavy pattern, not black. The female scaup is mostly brown with a paler brown-grey back and flanks, and a prominent white patch around the base of the bill. Both sexes show broad white wingbars in flight and have golden eyes. Scaup form large flocks, usually on shallow coastal waters.

- **SIZE**
  42–51cm (16½–20¼in)

- **BREEDING**
  Does not breed in British Isles

- **FOOD**
  Mainly molluscs, especially mussels

- **HABITAT**
  Shallow coastal waters in winter, Arctic tundra in summer

- **VOICE**
  Male gives soft, quiet cooing; female has harsh *'karr karr'* flight call, slower than that of tufted duck

- **DISTRIBUTION**
  Winter visitor to coastal waters, sometimes found inland

A robust bird with a rounded head, the male has a black mark at the tip of its large bill. This area is smaller than that of the male tufted duck.

Female

Large area of white at base of bill

Pale grey back contrasts with black stern and white flanks

Male

POCHARD *Aythya ferina*

A chestnut-red head and neck, black chest and pale grey patterned back and flanks characterise the male. The prominent black bill has a broad pale grey band across the middle. The female is mottled brown, darker on the crown, neck, breast and stern, tinged with pale grey on the back and with a pale mark by each eye. In flight, both sexes show indistinct greyish wingbars, while males have contrasting dark breasts and white underparts.

- **SIZE**
  42–49cm (16½–19½in)

- **NEST**
  Depression near water, lined with vegetation and down

- **BREEDING**
  Lays 8–10 greenish eggs in April–May

- **FOOD**
  Invertebrates, small fi and aquatic plants

- **HABITAT**
  Open water in winter, smaller, well-vegetate pools in summer

- **VOICE**
  Male gives soft wheezing calls; femal louder rasping calls

- **DISTRIBUTION**
  Winter visitor in large numbers; breeds in north in small numbers

Fine, wavy markings on the male pochard's grey back and flanks are visible only at close quarters. These skilled divers flock to open fresh water.

Diffuse dark and pale markings on head

Female

Conspicuous black breast and stern

Male

EIDER *Somateria mollissima*

Male eiders have a noticeable pied pattern and a broken lime-green patch on the neck. Females are brown with darker barring and mottling. Large flocks of eiders gather on shallow coastal waters, flying low in long irregular lines or loose packs, looking heavy with drooping necks and using slow wingbeats. The ducks dive frequently. Females often guard the young in crèches, while males move offshore to moult.

● **SIZE**
50–71cm (20–28in)

● **NEST**
Depression near shore, lined with grass and thick down

● **BREEDING**
Lays 4–6 greenish eggs in May–June

● **FOOD**
Mainly marine molluscs, especially mussels, plus other invertebrates and some small fish

● **HABITAT**
Cool coastal waters

● **VOICE**
Mainly silent, but in breeding season male makes far-carrying, deep 'ah-ooooo' calls and female gives harsh calls

● **DISTRIBUTION**
Breeds around coasts of northern Britain and Ireland; winter visitors arrive from farther north

The eider has a distinctively shaped head and bill, not shared by other common diving ducks.

Marbled brown plumage

Female

Plumage black and white except when in moult

Male

COMMON SCOTER *Melanitta nigra*

The male common scoter is entirely black apart from a narrow yellow patch on top of the bill. The female is dark brown with obvious pale cheek patches. In winter, scoters are found in large flocks on coastal waters, but usually not where conditions are very rough. They swim buoyantly and dive well, frequently in search of molluscs. These ducks fly in large flocks, often in long, straggling lines, but sometimes in tight groups with a few stray birds following behind.

● **SIZE**
44–54cm (17½–21½in)

● **NEST**
Depression near water, lined with grass, moss and down

● **BREEDING**
Lays 6–8 cream eggs in April–June

● **FOOD**
Mainly aquatic molluscs

● **HABITAT**
Coastal waters in winter, upland moors and tundra in summer

● **VOICE**
Mostly silent, but makes whistling, hooting or grating calls in breeding season

● **DISTRIBUTION**
Large numbers settle around coast in winter; rare breeding bird in Britain

The yellow on top of the male common scoter's bill can be seen at close range.

Conspicuous pale cheeks

Female

Bill yellow and black with a knob at its base

Male

VELVET SCOTER *Melanitta fusca*

Superficially like the smaller common scoter, the male differs in having white eye patches and a larger yellow patch extending on to the sides of the bill. The female is almost all dark brown, but with two white patches on the face. Both sexes show a broad white bar on the inner hind wing in flight, or when flapping their wings on the water. Sometimes small flocks may mingle with much larger flocks of common scoters, but are slower to take flight.

● **SIZE**
51–58cm (20¼–23in)

● **BREEDING**
Does not breed in British Isles

● **FOOD**
Mainly aquatic molluscs, plus some crustaceans, other aquatic animals and plant material

● **HABITAT**
Coastal waters in winter, moors and tundra in summer

● **VOICE**
Usually silent, but male may make growling or whistling calls

● **DISTRIBUTION**
Winter visitor, mainly on North Sea coasts

A velvet scoter is appreciably larger and more robust than the similar common scoter.

Pale spots on cheek and at base of bill

Female

White patch under eye

Male

GOLDENEYE *Bucephala clangula*

A small diving duck, the male is mainly white with a black back, narrow black lines angled over white flanks, a glossy green head, and a rounded white patch in front of each golden eye. The female is mainly grey with a chocolate brown head, golden eyes and a pale patch at the tip of the bill. Small groups of goldeneyes visit estuaries, sheltered bays and lakes in winter, swimming buoyantly and diving frequently.

A male goldeneye displays to a female by tossing his head backwards. As with most ducks, courtship displays and pair formation are common in winter.

● **SIZE**
42–50cm (16½–20in)

● **NEST**
Hole in tree, high up, lined mainly with down

● **BREEDING**
Lays 8–11 bluish green eggs in April–May

● **FOOD**
Aquatic invertebrates, small fish and some plant material

● **HABITAT**
Lakes, estuaries and bays in winter, wooded lakes and rivers in summer

● **VOICE**
Normally silent but has rattling display call in spring; wings make a loud, rhythmic whistling

● **DISTRIBUTION**
Widespread winter visitor; about 100 pairs breed in pine forests in Scotland

Conspicuous chocolate brown head

Female

Hump on head contains air chambers, facilitating long dives

Male

LONG-TAILED DUCK *Clangula hyemalis*

The male of this small sea duck has a long, pointed black tail and pied plumage. In summer, the back and chest are black and brown. The black bill has a broad pink band. The female lacks the long tail, and has variable brown and white plumage with an all-grey bill. Both sexes have large dark cheek patches in winter. Flocks may be seen off northern and eastern coasts, often in very rough water.

The male is easily identified by his unmistakable tail, which he shows off by raising his rear end in courtship displays.

● **SIZE**
40–47cm (16–18½in) not including male's tail

● **BREEDING**
Does not breed in British Isles

● **FOOD**
Mainly aquatic molluscs and crustaceans plus some small fish

● **HABITAT**
Coastal waters in winter, rarely inland, breeds on Arctic tundra

● **VOICE**
Males give frequent musical yodelling calls

● **DISTRIBUTION**
Winter visitor from Scandinavia

Marbled plumage   Female

Short tail

Long pointed tail

Male

Black-and-white plumage

GOOSANDER *Mergus merganser*

A large sawbill, the goosander can look black and white at a distance. The male has a white body suffused with pink in winter and a dark glossy green head. The female is mostly grey, paler below, and has a high-browed reddish brown head with a bulging, drooping crest. In flight, the male's inner wings are largely white, while the female shows a large white patch along the rear of the inner wing. Both have long, slender, hook-tipped, deep red bills with serrated mandibles.

The elegant male goosander has a simpler plumage pattern and a sturdier bill than the red-breasted merganser.

● **SIZE**
58–66cm (23–25½in)

● **NEST**
Hole in tree, nestbox or crevice, lined with vegetation and down

● **BREEDING**
Lays 8–11 whitish eggs in April–May

● **FOOD**
Mainly fish, plus small mammals and insects

● **HABITAT**
Lakes, large rivers and reservoirs

● **VOICE**
Normally silent, but male makes muffled, ringing courtship calls from late winter

● **DISTRIBUTION**
Breeds in northern and western Britain; much more widespread in winter

Reddish brown head contrasts with mainly grey plumage

Female

Hooked, red bill

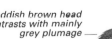

Male

RED-BREASTED MERGANSER *Mergus serrator*

This elegant sawbill resembles a grebe, with its slim build and slender bill, but it has an untidy divided crest. Males have a red bill, eyes and legs, white collar, black-spotted chestnut breast, glossy dark green head and finely lined grey underparts. Females are pale brown-grey all over, especially below, with a reddish head and small crest. Mergansers can be seen on coastal waters in winter, sometimes standing on shingle bars.

● SIZE
52–58cm (20½–23in)

● NEST
Concealed depression lined with grass, leaves and down, near water

● BREEDING
Lays 8–10 buff-olive eggs in April–May

● FOOD
Mainly fish

● HABITAT
Winters on coastal waters, estuaries, large lakes; breeds near northern lakes and rivers

● VOICE
Males have long, wheezy or rattling courtship calls; females give harsh croaking calls

● DISTRIBUTION
Winters on most British coasts, breeds in north-west

A female red-breasted merganser lacks the female goosander's sharp divide between the reddish head and pale throat.

Reddish brown head and shaggy double crest on nape

Female

Spiky double tuft

White collar

Male

SMEW *Mergus albellus*

A small species of sawbill, the smew appears mostly white but the male has black eye patches, dark slashes near the back of the head, black lines on the body and grey lines on the flanks. The greyer female is more grebe-like, with a reddish brown cap, dark eye patches and white cheeks. Juveniles resemble females, and most winter birds seen in Britain are 'redheads' – females or juveniles. Both sexes have short, narrow bills with serrated edges, and display white wing bars in flight.

● SIZE
38–44cm (15–17½in)

● BREEDING
Does not breed in British Isles

● FOOD
Mostly small fish, plus aquatic insect larvae

● HABITAT
Large lakes, reservoirs, sheltered coasts and estuaries in winter; wooded lakes in far northern Europe, Russia and Siberia in summer

● VOICE
Male has grunting or rattling courtship calls; female has various hoarse rattling calls

● DISTRIBUTION
Scarce winter visitor, mainly in south and east

Adult females and juveniles of both sexes are difficult to distinguish. They all have a russet cap and white cheeks.

Reddish head

Female

Mainly white with black markings and delicate grey patterns on flank

Male

RUDDY DUCK *Oxyura jamaicensis*

This small diving duck resembles a little grebe due to its compact shape and frequent short dives. The male is very distinctive with a brilliant blue bill, white cheeks, black head and neck and bright reddish brown body. Females are mostly grey-brown with a darker head and pale cheeks. The name 'stifftail' describes its distinctive habit of cocking its comparatively long tail. Males perform chest-beating displays, creating patches of bubbles in the water around them.

● SIZE
35–43cm (14–17in)

● NEST
Platform of reeds, rushes and leaves, hidden among waterside vegetation

● BREEDING
Lays 6–10 whitish eggs in April–May

● FOOD
Aquatic insects, snails, worms, seeds and grain

● HABITAT
Shallow lowland lakes and large rivers with rich plant life

● VOICE
Mostly silent except in display, when female makes high whistles and male makes rattles and croaks

● DISTRIBUTION
North American native, now well established in the south

The male's bill resembles blue plastic, and is unique among birds seen in Britain.

Female

Brown and white facial stripes

Black head with striking white cheeks

Rich chestnut plumage

Male

The snipe

Adept at probing deeply into mud and wet soil for food, the secretive snipe is a bird of rainswept moors, wild wetlands and coastal marshes. Few waders keep a lower profile, or reveal their presence quite so dramatically when alarmed.

A close encounter with a snipe is nearly always a startling experience. Having stayed hidden in low, damp vegetation until it is in danger of discovery, it bursts up with a harsh call of alarm. Jinking and swerving, it flies rapidly up and away, often rising high into the air, before diving back down into cover at a safe distance. It all happens so quickly that the bird rarely provides more than a confused impression of brownish plumage, a pale belly, flickering wings and a long, pencil-like bill. Its zigzagging aerial escape is enough to identify it as a snipe, but leaves no time for more detailed observation.

Luckily, snipe can also be seen in more leisurely circumstances, especially in winter when they occur in all sorts of damp places, including the relatively open margins of wetland pools, rivers, lakes and reservoirs, and by the brackish creeks of coastal salt marshes. A snipe will not tolerate a close approach, slipping into cover at the first sign of danger, but binoculars reveal a small, short-legged, rather dumpy-looking bird, mottled brown with pale buff streaks, with an extremely long, straight bill. It has the longest bill, in proportion to its size, of any bird in Europe, and this helps to distinguish it from its smaller, shorter-billed relative, the similar but much scarcer jack snipe.

Probing bill

The extra-long bill of the snipe is the key to its way of life. It is highly adapted for probing for prey in mud or soft, wet soil, and this restricts it to places where the ground is wet enough to be penetrated easily, and where small animals, such as worms and insect grubs, are numerous. This rules out most arable land, which is too well drained and often laced with pesticides, but snipe are often encountered on marshy riverside meadows and damp pasture, especially when winter flooding creates large areas of standing water.

▲ Once in the air, the snipe flies fast on pointed wings, with its long bill angled downwards. Its zigzagging flight style as it escapes danger is very distinctive.

◄ The combination of a very long, straight bill and pale creamy buff streaks on the back is unique to the snipe. The only other birds with similar features are the smaller jack snipe and the much bigger woodcock.

SNIPE FACT FILE

Small, skulking and exquisitely camouflaged, the snipe is one of the most elusive of waders. It is rarely seen in the open except at long range, but a good view reveals the subtle beauty of its plumage and the extraordinary length of its bill.

● NAMES
Common names: snipe, common snipe
Scientific name: *Gallinago gallinago*

● HABITAT
Wetlands and damp grassland; also river and lake margins, drainage ditches and coastal salt marshes in winter

● DISTRIBUTION
Throughout Britain and Ireland; absent from the far north and west of Scotland in winter

● STATUS
Probably around 30,000 pairs breed in Britain, and around 10,000 in Ireland; in winter, numbers are swelled by perhaps as many as 100,000 migrants from Europe

● SIZE
Length 25–28cm (10–11in), of which the bill is about 7cm (2¾in); wingspan 37–43cm (14½–17in); weight 80–120g (2¾–4¼oz)

● KEY FEATURES
Smallish but stocky wader with a very long, straight bill and short legs; buff and blackish stripes on head, bold, creamy buff stripes on mottled brown back, buff breast with dark brown arrow marks, white underparts with dark bars on flanks; buff stripes on back show up well in flight, which also reveals white trailing edge to wing and short tail with white band at tip

● HABITS
Mostly secretive, feeding in cover of dense, low-growing vegetation, bursting up with twisting escape flight if approached too closely; may feed in the open, sometimes in small groups; in breeding season, perches on conspicuous mounds or posts to sing, and males perform spectacular 'drumming' display flights

● VOICE
A rasping '*scaaap*' of alarm; rhythmic, repeated '*chipp-er chipp-er chipp-er*' in breeding season

● FOOD
Mainly small invertebrates, including earthworms, insects (both adults and larvae), molluscs and crustaceans, plus some seeds and other plant matter

● BREEDING
Migrants start to return in February and March, with the last arriving by mid-May; eggs laid from early April to August; usually 1 brood, sometimes 2

The mottled, greenish brown coloration of the eggs acts as excellent camouflage, helping to protect them from predators.

● NEST
Shallow scrape on ground, usually in cover of vegetation such as grass tussocks, lined with fine grasses

● EGGS
3–5 (usually 4), pale green to olive with reddish brown blotches, incubated by female for 18–20 days

● YOUNG
Chicks follow their parents soon after hatching; initially they are fed by both parents, the brood split between them; the young fledge and become independent at 19–21 days old

High-set eyes give good all-round vision for defence, even when the snipe is probing deep in the soil.

A blackish stripe through the eye contrasts with a buff stripe above.

Bold, creamy buff stripes on the back show up well on the ground and in flight.

Almost twice as long as the bird's head, the bill has a soft, sensitive, mobile tip.

Distribution map key

■	Present all year round
■	Present during summer months
■	Present during winter months
□	Not present

Its legs are shorter than those of most waders.

PROTECTED!

The snipe is defined as a game bird under Schedule 2, Part 1 of the Wildlife and Countryside Act, 1981, which means that it can be legally shot at certain times of year. However, shooting a snipe during the close season of 1 February to 11 August is an offence.

The snipe's feeding technique is to probe the soft or flooded ground in a series of rapid stabs, pushing its bill right in each time. The bill tip is very sensitive, owing to a concentration of touch receptors and special sense organs that can detect pressure changes in the wet ground. These sensors give the snipe the ability to locate prey that may be some distance away, and quickly withdraw and stab down in the appropriate place to seize it.

To achieve this, the snipe must open its bill slightly while it is in the ground. The job is made easier by a flexible upper mandible, which enables the bird to open the tip of its bill instead of the whole length. It also has an extra-long tongue, which it can use to secure a worm and draw it into its mouth. This enables it to swallow prey without removing its bill from the ground – something that most other long-billed waders cannot do.

Feeding head-down like this leaves the snipe vulnerable to attack, but its eyes are set well back on its head, allowing it to scan all around and above for danger, even when probing deep into the mud. Even so, it prefers to feed at dusk and in the early part of the night, or at dawn, and spend the daylight hours resting or preening near the edge of the water. It relies heavily on its plumage to conceal it from enemies, and often avoids notice by crouching low in cover rather than flying off.

Winter visitors

In winter, snipe tend to gather in small groups on areas of soft, wet ground where they can feed intensively on burrowing worms, insect larvae and other prey. If icy weather strikes and the ground freezes, they move to the edges of streams and

Feeding in soft, wet mud enables the snipe to open its bill easily to seize prey, such as aquatic insect larvae.

rivers to feed in the shallows, where the flow helps prevent ice formation. If the stream margins freeze, prey may become very hard to find. A snipe that has fed well in the preceding weeks can survive on its fat reserves for a week, but no longer, so birds that breed in the far north are quick to move south and west as winter closes in.

This brings large numbers of migrant snipe to the milder lowlands of Britain. Some fly south from northern Britain,

but most are from Iceland, the Faeroes, Scandinavia, the Low Countries, central and eastern Europe and Russia. Individual snipe often visit the same areas year after year, swelling the resident breeding populations and spilling out on to seasonal wetlands that are never used as breeding sites. These migrants stay until late February and March, when they start to return north and east to re-occupy their own breeding grounds.

During the day the snipe often spends a lot of time caring for its plumage, bathing in the shallows and then preening the feathers back into shape with its bill.

SNIPE CALENDAR

MARCH ● MAY

Males return to their breeding grounds and claim territories with repetitive songs from prominent perches. At dawn and dusk they circle and dive through the air in display flights.

JUNE ● AUGUST

The chicks are highly developed when they hatch, and soon find their own food. Within three weeks the young birds have their streaked adult plumage, and are able to fly.

SEPTEMBER ● NOVEMBER

When breeding is over, many snipe move to lowland marshes. These include migrants from Iceland and the Baltic region, forced south and west by harsh winter conditions.

DECEMBER ● FEBRUARY

For those snipe that stay in colder regions of Britain throughout the year, the ice-free mud at river margins provides access to vital food when the nearby marshes and pastures are frozen.

Diving males

For most of the year snipe are inconspicuous birds, but in spring they lose their habitual caution and start displaying openly, often perching on prominent posts to utter their loud, rhythmic '*chipp-er chipp-er chipp-er*' territorial song. In the early morning and in the evening twilight the males take to the air above their nesting grounds to perform dramatic aerial displays. Rising high in the sky, each one circles widely and then dives with its tail fanned out so the stiff outer tail feathers project at right angles to the body. During the high-speed dive, air flowing over the projecting feathers makes them vibrate with a strange throbbing hum that seems to fill the warm air.

A displaying male will attempt to mate with any female that enters his territory. The female then nests on the ground in a grass-lined scrape concealed in a clump of vegetation. She usually lays four eggs, and starts incubating when the last is laid to ensure they all hatch at once. At this

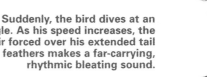

At dusk or dawn the male snipe rises high over his breeding territory on the boggy ground below, and flies in broad, undulating circles with fast, flickering beats of his pointed wings.

Suddenly, the bird dives at an angle. As his speed increases, the air forced over his extended tail feathers makes a far-carrying, rhythmic bleating sound.

Drumming display

On warm evenings in spring and summer, the male snipe claims his territory with a unique display flight, which also advertises his willingness to mate with any passing female.

JACK SNIPE

The snipe is easily confused with its smaller, more compact relative, the jack snipe *Lymnocryptes minimus*. The two frequent the same habitats and have similar plumage, but the jack snipe has broader, more obvious buff stripes on its back, dark stripes rather than bars on its flanks, and no central pale stripe on its crown. The most obvious difference, however, is its much shorter bill.

When seen in the open by daylight – which is rare – the jack snipe displays a curious habit of bobbing up and down on the spot. It is even more secretive and skulking than the snipe, usually staying hidden until it is about to be stepped on. When it does fly up, it does so without calling, and usually lands quite close by after a brief, low, direct flight. It is a winter visitor from the far north, seen only between September and April in lower-lying areas of England, Wales, southern Scotland and Ireland. Some 50,000 birds may visit Britain each year, but it is such an elusive bird that its true numbers are hard to determine.

Jack snipe often feed near snipe, but are much harder to see on the ground.

point the male rejoins her to help care for the chicks, although they are soon able to find their own food. The parents divide the brood between them, leading them to good feeding spots and defending them from enemies, if necessary by feigning injury to distract potential predators. When the young are able to fly, at about three weeks old, they disperse, gathering in small groups that may combine into large flocks before migration.

Lowland decline

The snipe once bred throughout the uplands and marshy lowlands of Britain, but over the last century or so the drainage of wet farmland has destroyed much of its lowland breeding habitat. It enjoyed a recovery during the agricultural slump of the early 20th century, but a serious decline began in the 1950s, especially in southern England where the intensification of agriculture has been most marked. Snipe have even declined in Ireland, formerly a stronghold of the species. Today most lowland-breeding snipe occur in protected wetlands, but the total area of these reserves is very small compared to the broad tracts of drained farmland that separate them.

Despite this, snipe are still numerous in the lowlands in winter, and some of these birds may be encouraged to stay on and breed by recent conservation schemes. These offer farmers incentives to retain and even recreate the wet grasslands that snipe use for nesting. If enough farmers take up the challenge, the strange, wild, thrilling display flight of the snipe could once again become a widespread and even familiar experience.

At first the adults feed the chicks bill to bill, each taking charge of half the brood, but the young are soon able to feed themselves.

WILDLIFE WATCH

Where can I see snipe?

● In winter, use binoculars to scan the edges of pools in marshy wetlands. Snipe can sometimes be seen feeding in the shallows, but they often simply sit near the water's edge.

● During the breeding season the best places to find snipe are wet moorlands. Stay out until dusk to get a chance of seeing – and hearing – the strange aerial display of the male.

● Keep a look-out for snipe on wetland nature reserves, especially those owned by the RSPB and the Wildfowl and Wetlands Trust. These reserves are often managed in ways designed to encourage breeding waders.

Rainbow trout

Cool, clean rivers and lakes are the preferred haunts of rainbow trout but this fish has adapted to living in warmer, shallower surroundings and its iridescent flanks bring a flash of colour to grey winter waters.

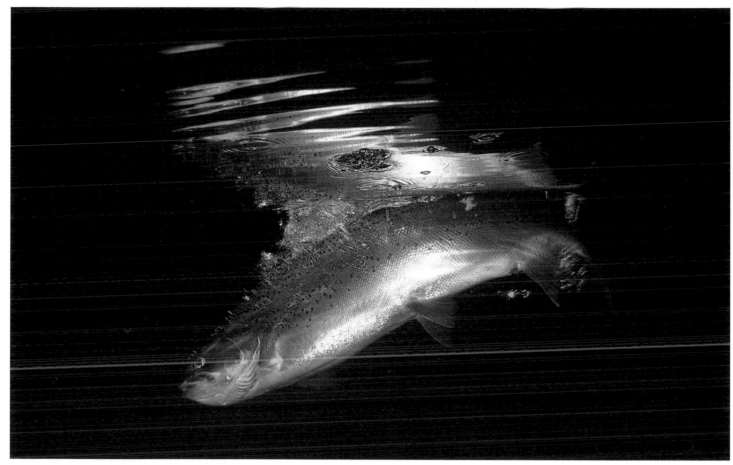

Most fish that live in lowland lakes are members of the carp family. However, another species that is also often found there is just as well adapted to life in still water, and that is the rainbow trout.

A native of the lands around the North Pacific, the fish's natural home extends from Alaska down to Baja California in Mexico, and, on the Asian side, from the Bering Strait down to the mouth of the Amur River. The rainbow trout has been introduced in many countries around the world and is now found on every continent except Antarctica.

The first live rainbow trout eggs reached England in 1884, and it soon became apparent that the species was more tolerant of poor water quality and relatively high water temperatures than the native brown trout, and furthermore was faster-growing. Inevitably, rainbow trout escaped from the waters to which they were introduced, and began to breed in the wild. In Britain and Ireland there are now about 40 naturalised breeding populations, although only eight of these are completely self-sustaining.

Game fishermen regard rainbow trout as a rewarding quarry and, as a result, it continues to be used to stock a wide variety of sluggish rivers, reservoirs and lakes that would be unlikely to support many native brown trout. Fish hatcheries have also been able to take advantage of the naturally variable breeding cycle of the rainbow trout to ensure that eggs are available for most of the year. This means that the fish can be raised to any required size at any time, making it ideal for fish farming.

Parallel species

In appearance, the rainbow trout is superficially like the brown trout, but rather more thickset. It is instantly identifiable, though, by the broad iridescent pinkish purple stripe that runs along each flank. Unlike the brown trout it has no red spots on its body, but it does

The rainbow trout has a silvery white belly and a beautiful 'rainbow' stripe down each flank. Its head is smaller and blunter than that of a brown trout, and unlike a brown trout it has spots on its upper fins.

have many black spots on both body and fins. In winter, it tends to feed more actively than the brown trout, and is more likely to be seen in still, shallow somewhat oxygen-deficient waters than its native counterpart.

The brown trout belongs to the genus *Salmo* and is closely related to the Atlantic salmon. Indeed, it occasionally interbreeds, producing hybrids that are quite common on some rivers. Until recently, the rainbow trout was included in the same genus, but it has now been reclassified as belonging to a different one, the genus *Oncorhynchus*, which includes all the species of Pacific salmon. In effect, it is the Pacific equivalent of the Atlantic brown trout, in both appearance and habits.

RAINBOW TROUT FACT FILE

Introduced to Britain for sport and as a food fish, the rainbow trout is now regularly seen swimming wild in rivers and lakes. It can tolerate poorer water conditons than the native brown trout, but rarely establishes populations that persist for more than a few years.

● **NAMES**
Common names: rainbow trout, rainbow; those that spend part of their lives at sea are called steelheads
Scientific name: *Oncorhynchus mykiss*

● **HABITAT**
Well-oxygenated, gravel-bedded streams, rivers, lakes and reservoirs

● **DISTRIBUTION**
Throughout British Isles

● **STATUS**
Numbers unknown; despite widespread stocking, successful spawning has been recorded in only a limited number of rivers

● **SIZE**
Weight of wild individuals up to 2kg (4½lb); escapes 5kg (11lb); stocked farmed fish up to 20kg (44lb) or more

● **KEY FEATURES**
Typically trout-like with second dorsal adipose (fatty) fin; back steely grey with black spots, belly silvery; bright pinkish purple stripe on each flank; tail fin heavily black-spotted; migratory steelheads bright silver on return to fresh water from salt water

● **HABITS**
Feeds mainly in open water, rising to surface to take floating insect prey; large fish feed mainly by night; a few populations feed at sea

● **FOOD**
Aquatic invertebrates, small fish and fish eggs, insects; large trout may eat frogs and small mammals

● **BREEDING**
Spawn mainly February–March on downstream slope of gravel shallows; eggs shed in shallow pit, male mixes in milt (sperm) to fertilise them

● **YOUNG**
Like small adults with dark blotches on flanks; fast-growing; breed for first time at 2–3 years

Young rainbow trout have a row of large, dark blotches or parr marks along each flank. The fish grow rapidly, reaching lengths of 10–15cm (4–6in) within six weeks of hatching.

Distribution map key

■ Present all year round

□ Not present

A rainbow trout's skin is covered with small, smooth round scales. Its dark spots and iridescence help to camouflage the fish on the gravel bottoms of fast-flowing streams.

The small dorsal fin is densely spotted.

Small black spots pepper the fish's silvery grey back.

Each flank has an iridescent stripe.

Like all salmonids, it has a small, fleshy adipose fin.

SPAWNING SUCCESS

If rainbow trout find a suitable breeding habitat, such as in shallow gravel-bedded streams, the females will spawn in early spring. They have similar requirements to Atlantic salmon, a coincidence that is thought to result in occasional hybrids between the species. However, male hybrids are always sterile.

The female rainbow trout sheds her eggs into a shallow pit – called a redd – that she digs in the stream bed. As the eggs settle among the gravel, a male will follow swiftly behind the female to fertilise them. The fertilised eggs then lie safely hidden in the gravel for 6–10 weeks – hatching time varies with temperature. The eggs are large and yolky, and each of the tiny fry – or alevins – hatches with a yolk sac attached to its body to sustain it.

Within a few days the fry are ready to start feeding themselves. They grow very quickly, and by the time winter arrives they are easily able to cope with the faster currents caused by increased rainfall.

◄ The eggs hatch at different rates depending on water temperature. The warmer the water, the faster they develop. The young are at their most vulnerable to predators – mainly other fish – at this stage.

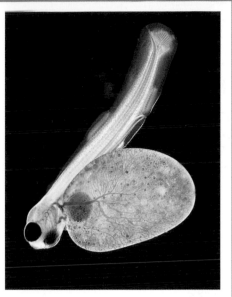

► Newly hatched trout such as this one are nourished by a yolk sac for their first few days. They develop into dark-spotted trout parr that hunt for their own food, feeding mainly on aquatic invertebrates.

Most rainbow trout are resident in fresh waters but some migrate out to sea at an early age, just like sea trout, and return to spawn in their natal rivers as magnificent, silvery steelhead trout.

Survival challenge

Although rainbow trout are notorious for their ability to escape from the confined waters of fish farms and lake fisheries, this aptitude is not matched by their survival skills. For generations in the wild, they inherited all the instincts necessary to survive, but now rainbow trout from controlled waters tend to be unable to recognise suitable places to live, find natural food in difficult locations or avoid predators. These are all skills that naturally spawned trout must be able to develop if they are to survive, and natural selection in the wild soon eliminates any strains that cannot rise to the challenge. By contrast, farmed fish are selectively bred for growth rate rather than survival skills, and most have probably lost the ability to produce offspring capable of surviving in the wild.

This accounts for the fact that, although escapes are common, and many British waters have been deliberately stocked with rainbow trout, self-sustaining populations of rainbow trout are rare. One of these occurs in the Derbyshire Wye, which was stocked with 750 yearling rainbows from a natural North American population in 1912 and 1913. These fish were effectively wild, so they had retained all their survival instincts. They found the rich, clear, limestone-fed waters of their new home ideal for colonisation, and were soon breeding. Wild brown trout and grayling populations along the colonised stretches appeared to decline, perhaps because of competition with the naturalised rainbow trout. However, declining water quality may have been the real problem, allowing the more pollution-tolerant rainbow trout to gain the upper hand.

Lake giants

Young rainbow trout feed on an invertebrate diet of mayfly and stonefly nymphs, caddis fly, midge and blackfly larvae, shrimps, water lice, snails and river limpets. In still waters, stocked fish often eat water fleas in large numbers, snails, and a variety of aquatic insects, including caddis flies, mayflies and damselflies.

They have large appetites, and in the right conditions they grow rapidly, achieving maturity at two years old and often reaching impressive sizes. Their natural lifespan is about four years, which is not as long as the brown trout. Most hatchery-bred rainbow trout released into rivers steadily lose body condition, and very few survive the rigours of winter. In the still waters of lakes and reservoirs, however, conditions can be less demanding, and huge, overwintered rainbow trout are often caught by anglers. Their growth potential has been demonstrated by a fish from Loch Tay in Scotland which, after escaping from a rearing cage, grew to a size of nearly 14kg (30lb) before being caught by an angler.

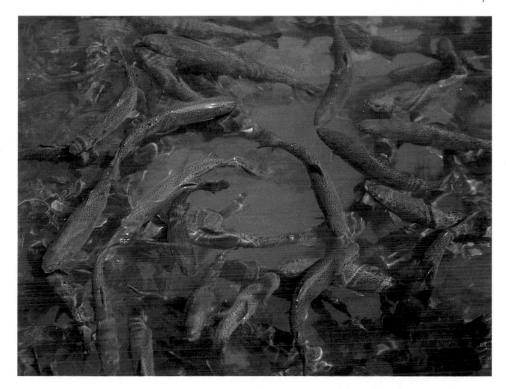

In still waters, rainbow trout will feed on a variety of invertebrates living on or near the surface. They will also take flying insects, such as spent mayflies, that have become trapped in the water's surface film.

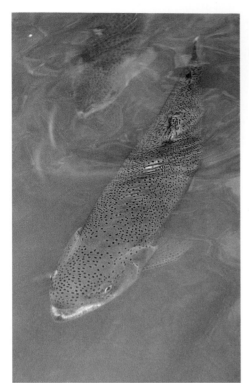

Surprisingly well camouflaged against a gravel-bedded stream, heavy-bodied rainbow trout cruise confidently near the surface. However, they are often taken by powerful predators, such as pike.

Such a rate of growth could be sustained only by a good diet, and big rainbow trout certainly have a reputation as predators of smaller fish, as well as other animals, such as frogs and even swimming rodents. The largest freshwater rainbows may prey almost exclusively on fish, lying in wait among aquatic vegetation and darting out to seize any fish that come within range. Migratory rainbow trout feed on fish at sea, as well as bottom-living invertebrates, such as worms and molluscs. On their return to fresh water to spawn, these sea-run trout may be more than 5kg (11lb) heavier than resident freshwater rainbows.

In their turn, rainbow trout provide food for larger fish. Native pike often flourish in lakes that have been stocked with rainbows. In two English lakes, the introduction of rainbow trout led to a doubling in the average weight of the resident pike. Small rainbow trout are also taken by birds, such as herons and cormorants, as well as otters and mink.

Potential threat

In North America, rainbow trout eat the dwarf land-locked Pacific salmon known as 'kokanee'. In the British Isles, escaped or naturalised rainbow trout are often seen as a threat to various native fish. Young salmon have been found in the stomachs of rainbow trout caught in chalk streams, and some authorities fear that they could eliminate vulnerable fish populations. This has already happened in other parts of the world. In South America, rainbow trout introduced to Lake Titicaca in the Peruvian Andes are thought to have destroyed stocks of native fish. Closer to home, populations of the local marbled trout in south-eastern Europe were seriously affected by introduced rainbow trout that both preyed on the native fish and competed with them for food.

Many people believe that it may be best to restrict the stocking of rainbow trout to purpose-built, isolated lakes, where they can do no ecological damage, and to leave river fisheries to the native brown trout. Others disagree, on the basis that rainbow trout have been living in British rivers for a century or more without any serious problems. In any case, the few populations that are truly self-sustaining are probably here to stay.

Although rainbow trout can tolerate warm, quiet waters, they may have little breeding success in those conditions.

The barbel

Specially suited to life in fast-flowing, lowland rivers, this native fish has a sleek, flat-bellied profile that enables it to hug the river bed and seize any small bottom-dwelling animals that are carried downstream.

During the daytime the barbel tends to keep to deeper water, where it is less vulnerable to predators, such as herons.

Strong, superbly streamlined and a determined, powerful swimmer, the barbel is a fish of fast-moving water. Its instinct for staying close to the river bed and its flat-bellied shape mean that it can keep as low as possible to take advantage of the way the flow near the bottom is slowed by friction. These adaptations enable it to inhabit waters that other species, such as bream, tench, carp, pike and perch, find intolerable. This reduces competition for food, and – in the case of pike – the danger of being ambushed and eaten. The barbel's natural habitat is the fast-flowing, gravel-bedded rivers of southern and eastern England, but it has been introduced to other English and Welsh rivers. It is absent from Scotland and Ireland.

Despite its shape, the barbel still has a battle to survive in its demanding environment, especially in winter when cooler water temperatures may make the fish much less active. Cold water is also more viscous than warm summer water, exerting more drag on the body of the fish and sapping its energy. During winter floods, when the current is strongest, barbel are often carried considerable distances downstream. Unlucky fish can even be swept into estuaries where they may die. They try to avoid this by congregating in slacks and eddies, in deep pools, or anywhere that offers some shelter from the relentless force of the current.

Quiet refuges

Even at other times of year, barbel prefer to live in places that offer some refuge from the main flow of the river. They favour tree roots and tree trunks, weed beds, boulders, rock ledges, bridge supports and the quiet waters under the sills of weirs. They move deliberately between these sheltered areas at different times of day, and as the river flow varies.

During the day, barbel usually occupy territories in relatively deep water, by sunken dead trees or undercut banks that provide safe cover, but at dawn and dusk they become more active, and venture out into shallower, faster water.

DID YOU KNOW?

At one time, barbel living in the Thames were caught for the table, and large numbers are still caught for food in eastern Europe. The fish must be carefully prepared because the eggs and possibly the flesh of spawning females contain toxins that can cause severe stomach pain. This is probably a defence against predators, as the females are most vulnerable when spawning.

BARBEL FACT FILE

The barbel is a distinctive fish, most easily recognised by the four long feelers – or barbels – that fringe its mouth. It has a powerful, streamlined, flat-bellied body that enables it to live in strong currents, and big fleshy lips for sucking up small animals from the river bed.

Two pairs of sensory whiskers are attached to the upper lip. These contain taste cells and touch-sensitive nerve endings to detect prey buried in the stream bed.

● NAMES
Common name: barbel
Scientific name: *Barbus barbus*

● HABITAT
Fast-flowing, middle reaches of clear rivers, with sandy or stony bottoms

● DISTRIBUTION
Native to east and south-east England, but widely introduced elsewhere; absent from Ireland and Scotland

● STATUS
Population unknown but not threatened

● SIZE
Length usually up to 50cm (20in), but can reach 1m (40in) or more; weight usually up to 2kg (4½lb), but can reach 8kg (18lb)

● KEY FEATURES
Flat-bellied and muscular, with sloping forehead; mouth with thick fleshy lips and two pairs of sensory feelers on upper lip; large pectoral and pelvic fins; broad, powerful tail; dorsal fin with rigid rays; shoulders bronze, blending to pearly white belly, fins coral pink; spawning male develops white nodules on head and back

● HABITS
Forms stable shoals; may remain in same stretch of river for life, but mature fish may make long-distance movements, settle, then return to original home territory; may live for 20 years or more, although few exceed 8–10 years

● FOOD
Bottom-living molluscs, crustaceans, worms and insect larvae; eggs and young of other fish and small adult fish, such as minnows or bullheads

● BREEDING
In spring large male-dominated shoals spawn over gravel shallows; depending on their size, females produce 3000–30,000 yellow eggs

● YOUNG
Newly hatched larvae are about 8mm (⅜in) long, with yolk sacs; drift into quiet river margins where they feed on small invertebrates; they reach 10cm (4in) after one year; males mature at 3–4 years, females at 5–8 years

Distribution map key

■	Present all year round
□	Not present

After a few months, young barbel leave the protection of the river margins and move into fast-flowing waters. Here they form small groups that hug the river bed as they adjust to the strong currents.

The first three to four dorsal fin rays are pointed and serrated.

A greenish brown back and bronze shoulders fade into golden yellow flanks.

Fringed with sensory barbels, the upper jaw juts beyond the lower jaw.

FEEDING FORAYS

Barbel prey mainly on invertebrates such as midge larvae, caddis fly, mayfly and stonefly nymphs, shrimps, snails, mussels and worms. They also take small fish, and large barbel may be distinctly predatory, regularly eating minnows, lamprey larvae, bullheads, stone loach and even small barbel that venture into adult territory. Despite this, a barbel has no teeth in the front of its jaws – all food is crushed and ground by bony 'pharyngeal' teeth, located well back in its throat, near the pharynx.

Feeding forays usually involve a series of stealthy moves upstream to investigate stretches of water that may be rich in invertebrates, each followed by a loop back downstream. By degrees the fish build up the confidence to occupy new parts of the river, and settle in to feed.

Their caution is well founded because barbel are regularly seized and eaten by herons, cormorants, pike and mink. Barbel sense their environment acutely through their eyes, nostrils, lateral lines and inner ears, and they are always alert to the possibility of danger. Large, old barbel tend to become excessively shy and live solitary lives. They may be active only at night, when they feel safe from danger.

◀ A heron is quite capable of catching a heavy-bodied barbel, although it may have to stab it and bring it to land first, before consuming it in small pieces.

▶ The diminutive stone loach emerges to forage at night and may make a good meal for a large, mature barbel. Although the barbel has no front teeth, its large mouth effectively sucks in its prey.

In faster-flowing water they actively prey upon insects and crustaceans, especially caddis fly larvae and shrimps.

It is probably no coincidence that at exactly this time of day, dawn and dusk, several invertebrates leave the safety of the stones to forage on the river bed. Barbel are well equipped for finding their prey in the low light, since their two pairs of feelers are sensitive to both touch and taste as they probe the gravel. Large barbel will take small fish when they can, and the young of larger species.

In deeper rivers, and especially during late summer when the water is warm, barbel may feed all day in undisturbed, swiftly flowing, gravel-bedded stretches of the river. This is particularly true of small to medium-sized barbel, which move around in tight shoals, often tucking under beds of water-crowfoot for temporary cover.

Before feeding, barbel often perform porpoise-like 'rolls' at the water surface. Several other fish of the carp family – the group to which the barbel belongs – do the same. This behaviour may be a way of making sure the blood is well oxygenated prior to actively searching for and digesting food – so it is, in effect, a warm-up exercise.

In Britain, most barbel grow only during summer, when the higher water temperatures stimulate their metabolism. Farther south in Europe they can keep growing throughout the year. Under these conditions they reach maturity more rapidly than in Britain, but they may not live so long. British barbel have been known to live for 20 years or more, although 8–10 years is more typical.

Ideal nursery
Spawning occurs throughout May and June. Both sexes migrate upstream to reach silt-free, unpolluted gravel shallows, ideally punctuated by deeper pools. Barbel eggs need to be laid in relatively clean, well-oxygenated water if they are to develop and hatch successfully. The spawning migration may involve a journey of several kilometres, or miles, particularly in rivers that have had many of their gravel shallows removed by deep dredging to improve land drainage. Unfortunately, this is all too common in lowland rivers. Where ideal spawning conditions and juvenile habitats no longer occur in the main channels of some rivers, some barbel populations migrate to particular tributaries where they can breed successfully in more suitable conditions. Radio-tracking studies have revealed that, after spawning, many adult barbel return to the stretches of river where they were living before the annual spawning migration.

By the time they reach the spawning areas female barbel are ripe with eggs. They are chased and chivvied by small groups of males, vying with each other to fertilise as many eggs as possible. The female fish turn on their sides and rapidly beat their tails to dig out shallow pits in the gravel. They then shed their sticky, yellow eggs into the pits, where they are fertilised by the males.

In spring, when barbel get the urge to spawn, large shoals may be seen migrating upstream. They may even leap up rapids in the same way as salmon, and groups of fish may be seen resting in sheltered eddies to recover from their exertions.

Gravel displaced from upstream may then tumble down gently to cover the eggs, helping to protect them from animals that might eat them. They need the protection because a long list of creatures – including leeches, flatworms, shrimps, stonefly larvae, some caddis fly larvae as well as most fish – will devour any exposed eggs. In addition, silty conditions can lead to mass mortalities through suffocation and fungal infections.

This is why mature barbel produce so many eggs. One female may lay up to 30,000 each year, but only two young fish need to survive to maturity to replace their parents in the population. It is possible that more than 99.9 per cent of individuals die before reaching breeding age. Mortality on this scale ensures that only the best adapted individuals survive and thrive. This must be why the adult barbels seen in rivers tend to be such superb specimens.

Even in clean rivers, young barbel are often scarce. This may be because they are vulnerable to predation, or perhaps because the necessary habitat for the early stages is limited. Juvenile barbel must have slack water along stream edges that are fringed with trailing vegetation. This allows them to adjust gradually to the rigours of life in fast-flowing water. Only after several months will the young barbel be strong enough to venture out into the main current and live among the stones on the stream bed.

Lake barbel

In a few places, such as reservoirs that are fed by water from adjacent rivers, barbel fry have been swept into still-water environments. Remarkably for a species adapted to fast-moving water, the fish have made their homes in the lake waters, and sometimes survive quite well. Growth

rates tend to be good compared to those of river fish, but the barbel may suffer in hot summers when dissolved oxygen levels in the warm, still waters are much lower than those in fast-flowing rivers.

Partly because of this, it is unlikely that successful spawning could take place in such still-water habitats. There is controversy over whether small angling lakes should be deliberately stocked with barbel, since the fish would be unable to establish self-sustaining populations. The lakes would have to be continually re-stocked, which might represent a threat to wild river populations.

Mature barbel may live in deep rivers, provided shallow, gravel-bedded stretches are available for spawning. Quiet areas are needed where young fish can stay until they are able to swim in strong currents.

Barbel are most active at night when they emerge to forage for bottom-living molluscs and crustaceans. They can sometimes be seen swimming in small shoals during the day, but usually remain in deep water.

WILDLIFE WATCH

Where can I see barbel?

● In winter, when rivers are in spate, barbel are often found sheltering in deep pools and quiet backwaters to avoid being swept away by the flow. At other times they prefer to feed in the current, and may even be seen in the turbulent waters at the foot of weirs.

● In early summer, watch for barbel migrating upstream to spawn. They travel in shoals, and may leap clear of the water to overcome obstacles.

● Look for spawning fish in gravel shallows. The large females are often escorted by small groups of male fish as they turn on their sides and beat their tails to excavate spawning pits.

The water spider

An ethereal-looking silver bell lodged deep in a pond may well be the home of this most resourceful spider – an air-breathing creature that has found ways of spending nearly all its life underwater.

eep below the icy surface of a pond in winter, an unlikely creature may be sleeping in a silken, airy refuge of its own construction – the water spider. Uniquely among its kind, this species spends most of its time beneath the water, where it hunts, mates, breeds and hides from the winter chill. Yet it has no special adaptations for underwater life apart from its instinctive ingenuity.

Life in a bubble

Like all other spiders, the water spider breathes air. It can survive underwater because it carries an air supply in the form of a bubble trapped by the velvety hairs on its abdomen. It does not simply swim about below the surface, however. It lives underwater in a much bigger bubble of air, trapped in a bell-shaped web that it spins among the water weeds.

The web starts out as a sheet of silk, but becomes bell-shaped as the spider fills it with air brought down from the surface. To do this the spider rises head-first to the surface and then flips over so that the tip of its abdomen and the tips of its legs just break through the water into the air. With

a sudden jerk it submerges its abdomen and legs, together with the large air bubble trapped between them. The spider swims or crawls down water plants to its bell and enters the web in a head-up position, releasing the bubble of air so it rises into the top of the bell.

The spider may need to make six or seven trips to the surface to fill the bell, but once it is filled, it can be almost self-maintaining. In well-aerated water, oxygen passes into the bubble by diffusion from the surrounding water as the original oxygen is used up. Oxygen released by water plants during photosynthesis may also be trapped by the bell. In poorly oxygenated water, oxygen diffuses out of the bubble, and this forces the spider to make regular visits to the surface to refresh its air supplies.

Aquatic hunter

Although closely related to the funnel-weavers, whose extensive sheet-webs often sprawl over low-growing foliage, the water spider is a true hunter. The web that it spins to trap air is purely a home, and plays no part in trapping prey, although

▲ The silvery appearance of the spider's personal air supply is caused by light being refracted through the bubble. This flash of silver is usually what first catches the eye, as the spider itself has a dark reddish brown body and legs. Other freshwater invertebrates, such as diving beetles, carry similar silvery bubbles of air.

▼ A water spider is structurally just like its land-living relatives. The closest of these include the familiar house spiders, which are able to survive underwater temporarily.

WILDLIFE WATCH

Where can I find water spiders?

● Water spiders occur all over the British Isles, as far north as the central Highlands of Scotland.

● They prefer weedy ponds and ditches and other still or slow-moving waters, including canals. Water spiders are abundant in many such places, although they do not occur everywhere. They are largely nocturnal, but sometimes swim in the daytime, looking like a silvery ball in the water.

● Try carefully dragging some weeds from a likely pond and examining them for spiders in a shallow dish, but don't take too many, and put them back quickly.

some of the strands of silk surrounding it may alert the spider to the presence of other animals. During the day it sits in its bell with just its legs sticking out, alert to any vibrations in the water that might indicate a likely meal. At night the spider usually ventures out in search of prey, often finding it by stirring up the sediment on the bottom of the pond. It preys mainly on aquatic insects, small worms and crustaceans, but occasionally eats young fishes and even tadpoles. It may also swim to the surface to investigate disturbances caused by airborne insects falling on to the water's surface film.

Seizing its victim, the spider stabs it with its large fangs to inject a paralysing toxin before taking it back to the bell to eat it. The spider cannot feed in the water because, like all spiders, it feeds by pouring digestive juices on to its food and sucking up the resulting solution. If it tried to feed in the water, most of its liquefied food would drift away.

Underwater nursery

Mating takes place in the female's bell in spring and summer. The male is often as big as, or bigger than, the female so, unlike the males of some other spider

▼ The water spider's air-filled 'diving bell' is firmly anchored to strands of water weed with silken threads to stop it popping up to the surface of the pond.

Its eight long legs enable the water spider to move easily through tangled aquatic plants, as well as swim in open water.

species, he is in no danger from her. He may mate with her several times before swimming off to look for another partner. After mating, the female lays 50–100 eggs, enclosing them in a white silk egg sac in the upper part of her bell. The eggs hatch in a few weeks and the babies gradually leave the bell. Some settle down and build their bells in the same pond, but others climb out of the water and allow the breeze to carry them away on tiny silk threads. The lucky ones reach new ponds.

As winter approaches, water spiders move farther down into the water and spin new bells with thicker walls. These bells are usually completely sealed, and the spiders stay inside them until spring, safe from the freezing winds and hungry hunters above the surface.

▼ When the water spider is building its bell, it stocks it with a series of extra-large air bubbles, which it carries between its abdomen and hind legs. Each big bubble makes it very buoyant, so it has to swim strongly to reach its destination.

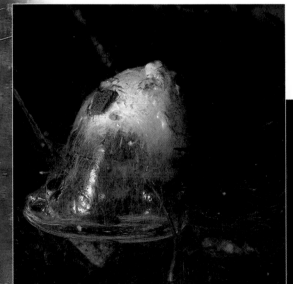

Ponds or slow-moving streams are ideal for water spiders. Fast-flowing water would dislodge the delicate diving bell. Well-oxygenated water is best, as the oxygen diffuses into the diving bell to replace the supplies used up by the spider.

Great pond snail

Thanks to its ability to store air, this large aquatic snail is able to survive in stagnant waters that contain little oxygen – but only if it can get to the surface to replenish its supply.

Like the more familiar land snails, the great pond snail clings to plants and other objects with its large foot, which is coated in sticky mucus. The muscle contractions that ripple along the sole of the foot make the animal glide forward.

In late winter, as the sunshine of longer days starts to penetrate and warm the waters of lakes and ponds, water snails emerge from their refuges in the mud. The most conspicuous of these aquatic molluscs is the great pond snail, the largest species of aquatic snail in the British Isles. In large lakes it may grow so big that it looks like a whelk cruising over the lake bed, but unlike this marine snail the great pond snail is mostly herbivorous, feeding on the algae that would otherwise smother aquatic plants, as well as organic debris and bacteria – although it may also eat fish eggs.

The great pond snail is easily identified by its large, pointed or spired shell. This is normally coiled clockwise and grows continuously when the snail is active, new layers being laid down around the outer edge of the shell opening. The shell is made of calcareous material, and a good supply of calcium in the water is essential for its growth. The great pond snail cannot live in very acid, calcium-free

waters. Growth tends to be fastest in summer, and slow or non-existent in winter, when the snail lies dormant in the bottom mud until sunshine warms the waters once again.

Primitive lung

The great pond snail is a 'pulmonate' species, which means that it has a primitive form of lung. Evidence of its distant relationship to land snails, the lung allows the animal to breathe air at the water's surface and store it in a cavity when it submerges to feed. This enables it to survive in stagnant water that contains little dissolved oxygen, and accounts for its scientific name *stagnalis*. The snail also absorbs oxygen from the water through its skin, especially that of its broad, flattened tentacles, so it can remain submerged in well-oxygenated water. If such waters ice over, or when the snail is hibernating in the bottom mud, it can get enough oxygen from the water alone, but if the water is stagnant it may die.

Despite its poor eyesight, the snail is able to explore its environment using other sense organs – tentacles for touch, and tiny cell-lined chambers that allow it to balance and to 'smell' dissolved chemicals in the water.

GREAT POND SNAIL FACT FILE

Largest of all the freshwater snails found in Britain, the great pond snail can be found in surprisingly small, shallow ponds, provided they contain enough food. The bigger the habitat, however, the bigger the snail may grow.

● **NAMES**
Common name: great pond snail
Scientific name: *Lymnaea stagnalis*

● **HABITAT**
Well-vegetated ponds, lakes, slow-flowing rivers, canals and streams

● **DISTRIBUTION**
Mainly calcium-rich waters in southern and central England

● **SIZE**
Height 35–60mm (1⅜–2⅜in; width 18–30mm (¾–1¼in)

● **KEY FEATURES**
Thin, variably coloured shell with long, pointed spire; last whorl very large; skin brown or grey; large head with long, flattened tentacles

● **FOOD**
Algae, plant material, organic debris and fish eggs

● **BREEDING**
Eggs laid in jelly on undersides of leaves, about 300 at a time; baby snails hatch fully formed

Distribution map key

■ Present all year round

□ Not present

Made of alternating layers of protein and calcium carbonate, the shell is very strong.

The tightly coiled apex is the oldest part of the shell.

Organic debris and algae is scraped up by the tongue-like radula.

The bodies of some water snail species are protected by a trap door, called the operculum, which closes the shell aperture. The great pond snail lacks this structure, but when hibernating it seals the mouth of its shell with a tough membrane to keep out the cold.

Muscle waves
Like all snails, the great pond snail moves on a trail of mucus secreted from the under-surface of its muscular foot. Waves of muscle contraction allow the animal to glide smoothly along, rasping the algal coating from plants and stones with the horny ridge-like teeth on its ribbon-like tongue, or radula. It locates food mainly by taste. Its two flattened, retractable tentacles have eyes at their bases, but the

snail's eyesight is probably only good enough to detect light and dark, and not sharp images. It avoids predators by retreating into its shell, but this may not save it from being swallowed whole by enemies such as roach and tench, or diving ducks, such as the pochard.

Like all pulmonate snails, the great pond snail is a hermaphrodite – each individual produces both eggs and sperm. Despite this, the snails seek mates and fertilise each other, laying their eggs in jelly-like masses attched to pond weeds

and stones. The eggs develop into tiny snails within the egg mass, and break free of their protective jelly when they are ready to fend for themselves.

The ideal habitats for great pond snails are large, moderately warm, calcareous ponds, lakes and rivers, which are free from suspended grit and organic pollution, and support plenty of aquatic plants. Unfortunately, such waters are becoming increasingly scarce as ponds and wetlands are drained, and many of those that remain become polluted by farm effluents, fertilisers and pesticides. So although the great pond snail is still a relatively common species, it is becoming less so every year.

▶ **After mating, each adult snail lays up to 300 eggs in sausage-shaped, gelatinous masses, stuck securely to the undersides of plants and other submerged objects.**

▼ **Within the egg-mass, tiny snails are developing. By the time they hatch they will be fully functional and independent miniature versions of the adults.**

WILDLIFE WATCH

Where can I see pond snails?

● This snail thrives in clean, well-vegetated ponds. Check the waters of any clear, healthy ponds for snails and other freshwater animals, such as newts.

● The snail has many relatives in the genus *Lymnaea.* Examine healthy ponds to see how many different species of snail they support. Other British species include *Lymnaea auricularia,* the ear pond snail; *L. glabra,* the mud pond snail; *L. palustris,* the marsh pond snail; *L. peregra,* the wandering pond snail and *L. truncatula,* the dwarf pond snail.

● There are many other types of freshwater snail, such as the attractive great ramshorn snail, which is shaped like a miniature fossil ammonite and lives in ponds. River and lake limpets are tiny cone-shaped relatives of the familiar, much bigger marine species.

Coast watch

- Otters by the sea

- The ship rat
- The common dolphin
- The herring gull
- The gannet
- Recognising coastal waders
- Barnacles
- The lugworm
- Sea mats

Otters by the sea

Some otters live along the coast all year round, while others visit when inland waters are in danger of freezing. They are most likely to be found along the shoreline of the sea lochs that abound in western Scotland.

If rivers and lakes freeze over, it becomes difficult for otters to dive and feed. When they succeed in reaching the water below the ice, they risk becoming trapped. If cut off from air, they soon drown. So for otters, one of the advantages of living near the coast is that the sea and its estuaries do not freeze, except at very low temperatures rarely experienced in Britain. The only drawback of salty water is that, over a long period, it causes the animals to become less buoyant, but otherwise they are well adapted to life on the coast.

Although estuaries are usually muddy, which can make it difficult for otters to move about, plenty of food is available – a combination of freshwater and sea fish. They travel from one tidal creek to another, leaving their characteristic webbed footprints in the mud. They also slide down steep mud banks, snow-covered slopes or sand dunes, creating a chute directly into the water.

Scottish retreat

The largest numbers of coastal otters are found off the western coast of Scotland and around some of the Scottish islands, where sheltered sea lochs ensure the waters are almost always calm. The lochs are protected from turbulent waves by rocky ridges offshore and by dense beds of seaweed. Here, the otters are in no danger from crashing waves, and flourishing masses of seaweed harbour abundant prey.

Otters find shelter and bear their young among the boulders higher up the shore, or they burrow in the soft soil above the beaches to make a den, called a holt. Many of these coasts have low cliffs, or none at all, making it easy for the otters to travel inland. The shore often slopes up directly on to grassy fields, so that they can forage in ditches and ponds on those occasions when extreme weather does cause the sea to be too rough.

With less danger from the agricultural chemicals that helped cause their decline elsewhere, the Scottish coast has one of the largest and most secure otter

As the tide drops, the seaweeds that cloak the rocky shore provide a rich feeding ground for the coastal otter. Without a deep covering of sea water, crabs and fish are easy targets for such an active predator.

PROTECTED!

The otter is afforded full legal protection under Schedule 5 of the Wildlife and Countryside Act, 1981. It is an offence to kill otters or disturb them or their homes.

populations in Europe. Today, there are probably more than 6500 living around the western coasts and isles of Scotland, which is more than half of all the otters in Britain. Over 1000 otters live on Shetland alone. In the best coastal sites, otters inhabit territories of 2–13km (1–8 miles). They often use sea caves and rock holes to rest when they are not hunting, particularly in daytime.

Seafood diet

From late autumn and through the winter, otters feed mainly on fish but, as the weather gets warmer, they consume more shellfish – especially crabs. As these are easy to catch and plentiful, the otters waste little energy in their pursuit. They do take quite a long time to crunch up, though, and there is a lot of indigestible 'packaging', in the form of the crab's hard outer skeleton, to be consumed. Despite its size, the average shore crab has relatively little meat. The fat edible crabs seen on the fishmonger's slab are too big and strong for otters to tackle. In any case, they are usually found in deeper waters where otters rarely hunt.

The alternative to relying on crabs is to catch more fish. Most fish are meaty and easy to swallow in a few seconds, so no time is wasted before the hunt for the next one can begin. However, although fish are desirable prey, they often lurk among the seaweeds, or hide beneath rocks or in crevices. It can therefore take an otter, searching around in likely places, some time to find them. Even then, fish move much faster than crabs, so they escape more often. Chasing fish, especially underwater, is hard work and requires an otter to use up much of its energy.

Slow-moving fish

The otter cannot afford to expend more energy catching its food than it derives from eating it, and a compromise is to

GROOMING AND WASHING

The saltiness of sea water is not a serious problem for otters but it does make their fur rather sticky. Otter fur usually holds a layer of air close to the skin. Although this makes them more buoyant so that they need to paddle energetically to stay under water, it also insulates them as they swim in cold water. Salty sea water causes individual hairs to become matted together so that air in the fur is lost.

Consequently, coastal otters need to spend more time grooming each day to prevent their fur from becoming clogged. They typically spend about 10–15 minutes hunting, followed by a longer rest period. During this pause, roughly half their time is spent grooming. Riverside otters that hunt in fresh water spend only around a quarter of their resting time in this way.

Grooming, and washing in fresh water, prevents salt from building up on the fur as it dries. Most coastal otters seek out freshwater streams and ditches in which to wash and clean the salt from their fur. In fact, stretches of coast that lack access to a source of fresh water do not usually support many otters. The coasts of Scotland provide plenty of places where streams come down to the sea, and rain-filled ponds are often found near the beach, so that the otters do not usually need to travel far.

Frequent grooming helps keep an otter's coat waterproof. Salt clogs the fur and decreases its insulating properties.

feed on slower fish, particularly eels, flounders and small flatfish, such as plaice. These are clumsy swimmers, as are heavy lumpsuckers. Male lumpsuckers are especially easy prey for otters from March to May, when the fish attach themselves to rocks and remain in one place, guarding the masses of eggs laid by the females. These fish cannot escape, so they are often easily caught.

For most of the year, coastal otters also prey heavily on the viviparous blenny. A rock-pool fish with an eel-like body, a fat face and bulging eyes, it can weigh up to about 20g (¾oz) – the same as a mouse. Although not very large, the viviparous blenny has plenty of flesh on it. Abundant in summer, these fish do not swim far and are relatively easy to catch. Five-bearded rocklings are also popular otter prey for similar reasons. They live in shallow water and can be quite big, weighing up to 200g (7oz).

On the upper shore of sheltered coasts, otters may find small seashore fish, such as common blennies and rock gobies. These are plentiful in spring and summer, and otters hunt for them in and beneath the damp seaweed blanket, or beneath rocks in shaded crevices. In summer, they also find various other fish that have been marooned temporarily in rock pools or in shallow pools on the shore.

Scorpion fish are common but spiky so that most predators avoid them. Otters do tackle them but take great care when

The otter family unit remains intact until the cubs are several months old and much of the time is spent together. The cubs are born in June but do not appear outside the holt until July and August.

As with all young predatory mammals, the hunting skills of an immature otter leave plenty of room for improvement. The growing cubs gain experience by trial and error, strongly driven by pangs of hunger.

HUNTING AT NIGHT

An otter catches its prey mainly by touch. It is helped by sight, but this is not its main means of finding food. Otters often hunt at night when this coincides with low tide. In the dark and underwater among dense seaweed, it is difficult for them to see anything at all. Even daylight can be gloomy in winter in the far north of Scotland, reducing how much otters can see. Feeling with their whiskers and sensitive toes is a much more effective way for them to find fish that are hiding among the seaweed and rocks.

Free from the disturbances that occur elsewhere, many coastal otters are also active during the day. This is not so much because they can see better, but because of the behaviour of their prey. Many rock-pool fish remain inactive during the day. They are easier to catch in their hiding places than when they are rapidly moving about, as they do at night.

Look out for coastal otters at dawn and dusk, especially at less remote sites at low tide when prey becomes more accessible.

eating them and often come ashore to do so. Lobsters also require careful handling, but occasionally otters are prepared to brave this crustacean's large and powerful pincers.

An adult otter needs to eat about 1kg (2lb) of fish per day. For an otter occupying an area where its diet is composed almost entirely of small rock-pool fish, such as butterfish, this involves much energy-sapping work. Butterfish are thin and weigh less than 15g (½oz) each. Otters, therefore, try to select the biggest and meatiest fish they can find.

Many sea lochs now contain large, floating cages full of salmon being raised for market. If otters start helping themselves to these, they become unpopular with salmon farmers and may be at risk despite their fully protected status.

Changing tides

Unlike river otters, those living by the coast have to cope with the tide changing every few hours. Otters prefer feeding at low tide, foraging in rock pools and hunting in the sea, in water that is too deep when the tide is in. Here, they may find larger numbers of fish as well as a wider variety of prey to feed on. At high tide, the sea covers areas that have been exposed to the air and hence harbour fewer edible creatures, especially fish. The incoming tide is often also rather rough, and turbulent waves make it more difficult for otters to search for prey, or to eat it if they do manage to catch it.

An otter will generally swim up to 50m (165ft) offshore, diving for up to 90 seconds in water that may be as much as 8m (26ft) deep. Otters have large lungs that give them a good supply of oxygen while they swim under water. When diving, their heart rate slows down so that they use up less oxygen. However, they do not travel for long distances beneath the water. Instead, they search small patches thoroughly – feeling their way with their moustache of stiff whiskers – and bob up

▲ A dozing otter is still aware of its surroundings and will slip quietly into the water if danger threatens. Coastal otters are generally much easier to see than those living around freshwater rivers and lakes, where there is more cover.

◄ The sleek and streamlined otter creates a long, narrow wake. It swims low in the water, so that often all that is visible from a distance are the ripples it makes.

◄ Holding its prey in its forepaws, this Shetland otter feasts on the nutritious meal of a lumpsucker fish. The waters surrounding these northern Scottish islands abound with prey for otters.

▼ The droppings – or spraints – of otters reveal clues to their diet. Those of coastal otters typically contain the remains of crab shells and fish bones, indicating a varied intake of food.

to the surface immediately above. In this way, an otter may catch a fish every couple of minutes, although on average about three-quarters of all dives are unsuccessful. Otters mostly eat while floating at the surface, but they sometimes take their prey back to the shore. Then they swim holding their catch in their mouths, gripped firmly between their teeth. They are most likely to swim to shore with larger items of prey or if they have cubs to feed.

Potential dangers

Like most other forms of sea life, otters are vulnerable to oil spills. Major oil facilities have been built around Shetland,

and the risk of shipwreck is ever present all along the extensive rocky coastline. Heavy crude oil spilled from tankers floats like a sticky syrup on the sea, but in the sheltered lochs it is not quickly or easily dispersed and may remain a hazard for weeks. If oil gets on to an otter's fur, the hairs become matted and no longer provide protection from the cold water. If otters swallow oil, they may suffer an unpleasant death as it poisons them.

Fish traps – especially 'fyke nets' – set traditionally to catch eels and other fish in shallow coastal waters are another hazard. If otters swim into them, as they are likely to do when trying to catch fish trapped inside, they may be unable to get

out. They have only seconds to find an escape route before, held below the surface and unable to breathe, they drown. Dozens of otters are killed in this way each year, even though it is now possible to fit the traps with special guards to prevent otters from getting in. These are very effective without significantly reducing the catch of fish.

A problem for otters along some coasts is that pesticides and other pollutants make their way up the food chain into fish, especially the fat-rich eels that are the otters' staple diet in many areas. Otters accumulate the toxins in their body fat. This may have no effect for a while, but as otters draw on their fat reserves in winter they become ill and unable to feed properly. Sometimes otters die as a direct result of poisons they have consumed by feeding on affected fish.

WILDLIFE WATCH

Where can I see coastal otters?

● While coastal otters can be seen all year, they are most likely to show themselves at times of least human disturbance. Dull, rainy days in winter are ideal for this reason, especially in early morning and late afternoon.

● For excellent opportunities to watch otters, visit the Shetland Isles. Fetlar to the north-east is arguably best of all.

● The Orkney Islands have thriving populations of otters, as do many islands in the Hebrides. The coasts of Skye are recommended.

● Look in areas with shallower water in sheltered lochs and bays. Calm sea conditions make it easier to spot ripples left by a swimming otter. To see otters fishing, visit at low tide.

This holt on Shetland – where it is known as a hadd – is typical of resting sites chosen by coastal otters. Close to the sea, but beyond the reach of high tides and gales, it provides a dry, safe underground haven.

The ship rat

Once the most common rat in Britain, the ship rat – also known as the black rat – is now one of the rarest mammals, found mainly in the Outer Hebrides. Active all year round, in early winter the ship rat is busy caring for late litters of young.

So called because they used to be particularly abundant on ships, ship rats were transported all around the world from their original home, probably in India, reaching Britain more than 1600 years ago. Over the centuries, the ship rat population increased by thousands – perhaps millions – as countless ships docked around Britain's coasts. An agile rodent, the ship rat scurried ashore along gangplanks or swarmed down mooring ropes. Many hid in bales of cotton from the tropics, or in boxes of manufactured goods from other rat-infested ports, to be off-loaded ashore. By the Middle Ages the ship rat was thriving throughout Britain.

Ship rats made themselves at home in stores and houses, particularly in dockland areas. As goods were traded between farms and villages and towns, so the rats spread. The ship rat found plenty of suitable places to live in dockside warehouses, farm buildings and thatched roofs. For centuries, every home in the British Isles was thought to have at least one resident family of ship rats. Even as late as the 1950s, these rodents were still common near the docks in large cities such as London, Liverpool, Hull, Cardiff, Glasgow and Belfast, where they could live in old buildings with false ceilings and double walls without being seen.

◄ A notorious stowaway since Roman times, the ship rat is able to climb even smooth vertical surfaces. After a spurt of activity it remains motionless to survey its surroundings.

▼ Large eyes and ears help the ship rat to find its way in the dark. It prefers to live in the top storeys and roofs of buildings – accounting for its other common name, roof rat – where it gnaws cables and pipes.

SHIP RAT FACT FILE

Smaller and less stocky than the vastly more common brown rat, the ship rat is distinguished by its darker coat and longer, thinner tail. It can leap prodigious distances – up to 15 times its own head and body length.

● **NAMES**
Common names: ship rat, black rat, roof rat
Scientific name: *Rattus rattus*

● **HABITAT**
Mostly indoors, especially in old warehouses and stores in docklands in large cities; grassy slopes and cliff ledges on islands

● **DISTRIBUTION**
Small, short-lived, transient populations in Liverpool, Southwark in London, Avonmouth and sporadically at other ports; otherwise virtually extinct on mainland; 230–400 on Shiant Islands (uninhabited by humans) in the Outer Hebrides; very few on Lundy Island in the Bristol Channel, and on Alderney in the Channel Islands

● **STATUS**
Very rare

● **SIZE**
Length (head and body) 10–24cm (4–9½in); tail equal or up to one third longer than body; ear about 2.5cm (1in); weight generally about 150–200g (5½–7oz)

● **KEY FEATURES**
Fur black or greyish brown, paler below; tail very long, scaly, significantly longer than head and body; ears big, pink and almost hairless

● **HABITS**
Mainly nocturnal; forms social groups; fast and agile, skilled climber; raids cereal stores

● **VOICE**
Loud squeaks when frightened or angry; also whistling, piping sounds and ultrasounds

● **FOOD**
Almost anything edible, especially grain and stored human foods; favours fruit

● **NEST**
Untidy mass of gnawed and shredded paper, grass, cloth or other soft material

● **BREEDING**
Mainly March–November; up to 5 litters, each averaging about 7 young, produced per year

● **YOUNG**
Paler and greyer than adult, otherwise similar, although smaller

● **SIGNS**
Oval pellets in small clusters, similar to droppings of brown rats but blunt at both ends (those of brown rats are tapered and often pointed at one end); greasy smears where animals squeeze through small gaps or brush past pale-coloured walls – the grease marks are distinguishable from those made by brown rats because they form a broken rather than a whole loop

Breeding almost throughout the year, ship rats produce litters of anything from one to 16 young up to five times a season – a potential total of 80 offspring per year. The young are born pink and furless, with their eyes and ears closed.

Long guard hairs cover the fur.

Large ears are almost hairless.

Distribution map key

■ Present

□ Not present

Thin and long, the tail is used as a counterbalance.

SHIP RATS AND THE LAW

Despite its rarity, the ship rat has no legal protection and there is little interest in providing it with any. It is listed as an undesirable alien species in the Wildlife and Countryside Act, 1981. This makes it illegal to release the ship rat into the wild.

Its slender body allows the ship rat to squeeze deftly through small gaps in the structure of buildings, enabling it to inhabit hidden spaces. Its natural instinct is to climb – in Europe, the ship rat actually spends much of its time in trees.

Soon after the arrival of the brown rat, from the early 18th century, the ship rat population began to decline gradually. It is unlikely that brown rats fought ship rats or, as has been suggested, killed and ate them. Stone buildings, effective sanitation and rat-proof food stores made life difficult for rats and the brown rat was better able to withstand Britain's cold, wet weather. Elsewhere in the world, particularly in the tropics, both rat species live together without the ship rat being displaced. The use of effective rat poisons sped up the disappearance of ship rats because the rats tended to live in buildings, where poison could be put down easily.

Shipwrecked rats

Away from cities, shipwrecks enabled ship rats to invade islands. For example, a German grain ship foundered off Orkney in 1939 and ship rats were able to set up home on the island, surviving until about 1970. Today, on the remote Shiant Islands, part of the Outer Hebrides, where ship rats were probably marooned from a ship wrecked nearby in 1900, as many as 400 ship rats may be living – more than on the whole of mainland

Stowaways aboard ships

Sea travel once provided ship rats with many feeding opportunities. Grain was carried in sacks that the ship rat's sharp teeth could tear open easily. Today it is carried in bulk in rat-proof containers, and there is increased vigilance against rats boarding ships or disembarking. Nevertheless, ship rats still live near ports and harbours, especially on offshore islands.

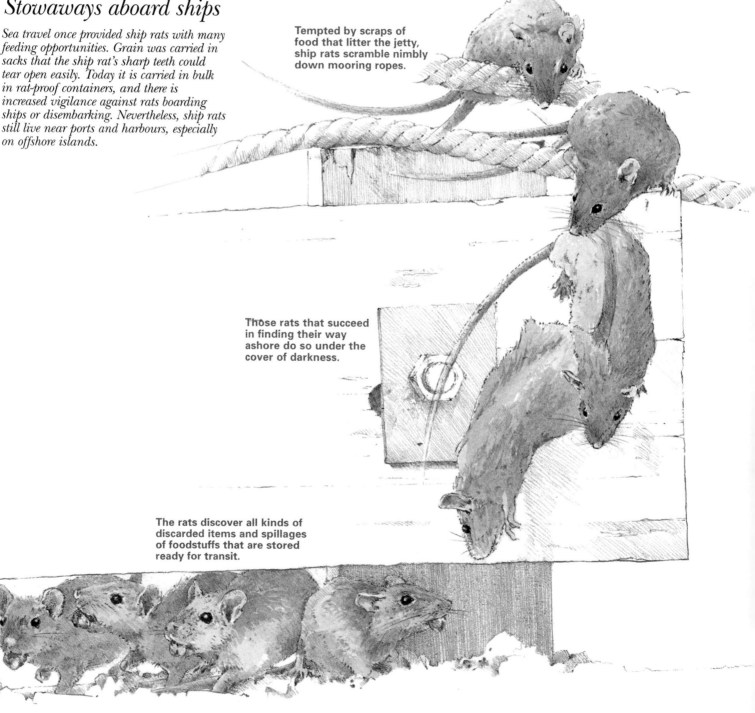

Tempted by scraps of food that litter the jetty, ship rats scramble nimbly down mooring ropes.

Those rats that succeed in finding their way ashore do so under the cover of darkness.

The rats discover all kinds of discarded items and spillages of foodstuffs that are stored ready for transit.

Britain. They also live on Lundy in the Bristol Channel, but numbers were reduced there in the early 1990s by a poisoning campaign. While they are rarely found out of doors on the mainland, ship rats on islands thrive among boulders and on rocky cliff ledges, despite being exposed to wind and rain. Their only shelter is in shallow burrows and lairs among stone walls, although they are sometimes found in and around buildings and rubbish dumps.

Agile climber

The ship rat can climb with great dexterity, using its forepaws and the toes on its hind feet to grip ropes and even thin telephone wires. Split wood, rough concrete or bricks or anything else that provides support, enables it to get into the highest parts of buildings, which are often inaccessible to human rat catchers. It is also able to swing upside down although, unlike the harvest mouse, it cannot use its tail to hang on to things. Instead, the ship rat uses its tail to balance, arching it from side to side in the way a tightrope walker uses a pole.

When frightened, the natural reaction of the ship rat is to leap and climb upwards. This contrasts with the brown rat, which tends to jump down to the ground and run away. On the ground, the ship rat travels in brief spurts of high-speed sprinting, then stops motionless to look around. It moves much faster than the brown rat and, being lighter and slimmer, can leap and climb with greater ease.

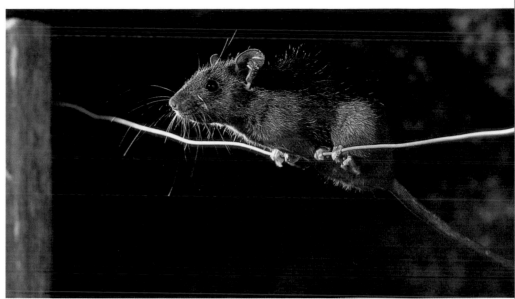

Ship rats have a superb sense of balance. Their long, mobile toes are designed for gripping and the long tail is used to aid balance, swinging from side to side or held lightly curled.

Social groups

Whereas brown rats swim well and often enter water, ship rats seem more reluctant to do so and prefer to live in warm, dry places. They form social groups that may be fairly small or comprise up to 60 individuals that occupy a territory around a feeding place. The territory usually covers only about 80–90m (260–295ft), although males may roam farther afield. Research indicates that ship rats have special scent glands on their cheeks and along their stomachs with which to scent mark their territory by rubbing tree branches and other obstacles.

◄ Male ship rats may engage in tussles over territorial boundaries, the dominant male being the most effective defender. Females are also often aggressive over food – much more so than female brown rats.

VARIED COLOURS

The ship rat is also called a black rat, because it is typically very dark in colour. However, many individuals are greyish brown, making identification difficult. There are two types of brown-coloured ship, or black, rats. One has a lemon yellow belly and the other is grey underneath.

These ship rats can look very much like the brown rat, *Rattus norvegicus*. However, ship rats, whatever their colour, always have a tail that is substantially longer than the head and body.

The group is dominated by a large male, sometimes with a hierarchy of subordinate males. Two or three top females are of equal rank. Although these are subordinate to the dominant male, they have authority over all the other members of the group. Both males and females are likely to warn away intruders. The females are more aggressive than the males, in particular towards female intruders. Fights are common but serious injuries are not. Most fights are instigated

► On the mainland, ship rats are almost invariably found in places where food scraps are left by humans. They prefer to live in warm, sheltered buildings, where they scurry about at night.

THE BLACK DEATH

The debate about whether the ship rat should be conserved in Britain is much influenced by its reputation for having spread bubonic plague in the past. Ship rats carry fleas to human households and rat fleas transmit the deadly bacterium that causes bubonic plague. Around 1340, a great plague swept through Europe causing sickness and death on a massive scale. Known as the Black Death, it wiped out whole villages and devastated countless families. A quarter of the population of Europe died, making the Black Death responsible for the greatest loss of human life in Europe prior to World War I. Three centuries later, the Black Death struck again. In 1665, over

97,000 Londoners died, and two thirds of these deaths were attributed to bubonic plague. If, as has been generally assumed by historians, the ship rat was responsible for the spread of this disease, it could be that its loss from the British Isles is desirable.

However, the question of whether the Black Death was actually caused by bubonic plague, spread by fleas that were carried on ship rats, is now a matter of controversy. A new study of the historical records of the Black Death of 1340 suggests that the rate at which it spread through towns and villages was different from the way that bubonic plague spreads. It may be that the Black Death was actually the

terrible result of some other highly infectious disease, such as anthrax, which spread in the unhygienic living conditions of the past. If so, then the ship rat and its fleas are not responsible. In various parts of the world, however, the ship rat is a known carrier of both plague and typhus.

The ship rat remains unwelcome in homes and buildings for other reasons – it gnaws woodwork, spoils food, chews sacks and paper to make its nests and leaves greasy stains where it squeezes through small holes or scrapes past immovable obstacles.

Rat flea
Xenopsylla cheopis
(Magnification x25)

The ship rat is host to a flea that carries the bacterium *Yersinia pestis*, which causes bubonic plague. However, a re-examination of the evidence suggests that the Black Death of 1340 may not have been bubonic plague after all.

by a more dominant rat towards a subordinate, and the losing rat soon runs away. Intruders and lower ranking animals often try to avoid trouble by being submissive.

Rats have sharp teeth with which they can inflict serious damage. Perhaps to avoid this risk, minor disputes are often settled by the animals barging against one another. Each opponent attempts to push the other off balance, using its haunches to shove its rival aside. Fighting ship rats may also stand on their hind legs and box one another with their front paws, jumping to avoid their opponent's blows.

Squeals and whistles usually accompany these aggressive encounters. Young ship rats are almost never attacked and can take food from under the noses of dominant adults without fear of reprisal.

Nocturnal foraging

Like the brown rat, the ship rat is omnivorous and will eat almost anything. However, it has a greater tendency to eat vegetable food, such as fruit and cereals, than does the brown rat. It eats about 15–30g (about ½–1oz) of food per day. Ship rats mainly forage at night and are especially active two or three hours after

sunset. However, they sometimes come out into the open in daytime if they are hungry and there is no noise or other disturbance to frighten them.

On the Shiant Islands, the eggs and chicks of puffins and other sea birds form part of the ship rat's diet. While the puffins are away at sea, the rats are likely to feed on dead birds, including the remains of puffins killed by great black-backed gulls. The rats also eat small invertebrates found on the shore, such as sand hoppers, and perhaps a few small crabs or molluscs. Seeds of the various plants that grow along the seashore form part of their diet as well.

Breeding behaviour

Most mainland ship rats never venture out of doors and are able to breed through most of the year in their indoor environment. The majority of young, however, are born between March and November.

The biggest and oldest females tend to have the largest families. A litter typically comprises around seven young, although it can be as many as 16, born after a pregnancy lasting three weeks. Female ship rats can produce up to five litters in a year, and are capable of breeding at

Although most urban ship rats are mainly black, some have brown fur, similar to brown rats. Among other distinguishing features, the long guard hairs on their backs and flanks give ship rats a shaggier appearance than brown rats.

12–16 weeks or when they have achieved a body weight of 90g (3¼oz). The young develop fast and are weaned after about 20 days. Few individuals live longer than one year, usually due to poisoning or being caught by domestic or feral cats, so breeding rates need to be high for a population to survive. In captivity, the longest-lived ship rat reached four years and two months old.

Brink of extinction

Until recently, a typical pattern would be for a few dozen ship rats to come ashore at a particular sea port but for them soon to be wiped out, while others appeared elsewhere. However, this scenario has become increasingly rare. Ships are inspected before they are allowed to dock, and effective poisons enable crews to keep their vessels rat-free. Mooring ropes and cables may have special metal cones attached to prevent rats from climbing aboard or leaving ships. Between 1981 and 1989, there were only a few hundred

ship rats left in Britain, and they were reported from just 23 locations on the mainland and a few islands.

It is now debated whether the surviving island populations of ship rats should be conserved or eradicated. Ornithologists would like to see the rats go because, in other parts of the world, they have severely affected sea-bird populations. Puffins and shearwaters, which live in burrows, are particularly vulnerable to rats taking their eggs and chicks. However, there is no evidence that ship rats actually reduce the populations of these birds in Britain. The puffin, for example, forms huge colonies on many rat-free islands off the Scottish coast. Even on the Shiant Islands, where ship rats thrive, there are about 80,000 pairs of puffins, and they are away at sea for most of the year.

▲ Due to their rarity, ship rats are sometimes kept in captivity, such as here at London Zoo. Under such conditions they are sociable animals, and mothers with broods of youngsters will rest together.

▶ Sacks of grain are easily nibbled to shreds by the ship rat's sharp teeth and the contents polluted with faeces. In the past, food stores were raised off the ground on mushroom-shaped pillars, called staddle-stones, to deter intruders.

▼ Despite its general avoidance of water, the ship rat lives in the vicinity of ports, although wherever it can, it remains almost exclusively indoors.

WILDLIFE WATCH

Where can I see ship rats?

● On mainland Britain and in Ireland the best chance of seeing ship rats is in zoo collections.

● On Lundy Island ship rats may be seen occasionally on grassy cliff slopes, but they rarely emerge until after dark. Lundy is also home to brown rats, which are difficult to tell apart from ship rats if glimpsed fleetingly.

● Small numbers of ship rats also survive on Alderney in the Channel Islands, and possibly Sark.

● The Shiant Islands, where the largest wild colony of ship rats lives, are privately owned and not easy to visit.

The common dolphin

One of the fastest and most acrobatic ocean mammals, the common dolphin is often seen off the west coast of Britain. These creatures frequently gather in large numbers to pursue schools of fish, swimming near to the shore.

Common dolphins belong to the order Cetacea, which includes other dolphins, whales and porpoises. These dolphins feed and breed mainly on the high seas but regularly venture into coastal waters in pursuit of fish shoals. So while they spend much of the year in the open waters of the Atlantic Ocean, they also patrol the western coasts of Britain and Ireland. This Atlantic seaboard is one of the best areas in Europe for watching large groups of common dolphins, and they are likely to be there at any time of year. They are noisy creatures, and their high-pitched calls and loud splashes mean the dolphins' approach is often heard before the animals can be seen.

Areas where upwelling currents bring prey to the surface – such as at the edge of the continental shelf that lies to the west of Ireland and the Outer Hebrides – are particularly attractive to common

dolphins. They generally prefer warm, tropical, subtropical or temperate waters, and those that live around Europe are dependent on the Gulf Stream. During the 1980s, the warm Gulf Stream current strengthened to the north, and common dolphins were found around the Shetland Islands off the north coast of Scotland.

Another stronghold for common dolphins is Gibraltar, which is surrounded by deep ocean currents, flowing from the Atlantic Ocean into the warm Mediterranean. The sharp incline in the sea bed up to the Rock creates the perfect feeding ground for common dolphins and they are present in the Strait of Gibraltar and Gibraltar Bay all summer. Large numbers of them use the bay as a stopover point for a few weeks at a time before swimming back to deeper waters offshore, just as they do off the west coast of Britain.

A speedy swimmer, the common dolphin may race over the sea with long, low leaps, its streamlined body slicing through the water. This behaviour is known as 'porpoising'.

Different types
There are two distinct species of common dolphins – the short-beaked and the long-beaked. While the most obvious difference between them is in the length and width of their beaks, there are other ways to tell them apart. The short-beaked species has a slightly chunkier body with a more rounded head, and lives mainly offshore. Spending most of its time inshore, the long-beaked species is slimmer with a more gently sloping forehead. The short-beaked common dolphin is the one seen in the seas around Britain and Ireland, as it makes forays inshore in pursuit of its prey.

COMMON DOLPHIN FACT FILE

Yellow and grey panels along the side of the common dolphin's body form an hourglass pattern, which may be noticeable when the animal rides a bow wave. That and its prominent beak disintinguish it from another common species, the white-beaked dolphin.

● NAMES
Common names: short-beaked common dolphin, long-beaked common dolphin, Fraser's dolphin, saddleback porpoise, white-bellied porpoise
Scientific names: *Delphinus delphis* (short-beaked), *Delphinus capensis* (long-beaked)

● HABITAT
Mainly offshore, but also coastal waters and continental shelf

● DISTRIBUTION
Short-beaked present all around British Isles but mainly off south-west coast of England and Wales and approaches to English Channel; also northern part of Irish sea, off west coast of Scotland and North Sea

Common dolphins require sustained international protection and are fully protected in British waters under Schedules 5 and 6 of the Wildlife and Countryside Act, 1981. This states that they may not be injured, killed, captured or removed when dead without a licence. There are also local regulations to inhibit boat operators from harassing cetaceans.

● STATUS
Abundant worldwide in temperate and tropical waters, but population in decline due to targeted fishing and accidental trapping in nets

● SIZE
Length 1.7–2.5m (5ft 10in–8ft 2in); weight around 70–110kg (155–242lb), males slightly heavier

● KEY FEATURES
Dorsal fin pointed, sometimes marked with white or pale grey on sides; hourglass pattern of tan or yellowish grey, black and white on sides and underparts; beak black and slender in long-beaked form, stubbier in short-beaked; flippers, dorsal fin and tail flukes black or grey

● HABITS
Playful, often rides vessels' bow waves; well-defined migrations not known; seasonal shifts off British Isles may be correlated with prey movements

● VOICE
Can be very noisy; high-frequency clicks, whistles and pulsed calls; squealing calls can sometimes be heard from above water surface

● FOOD
Small shoaling fish such as mackerel, flatfish and squid

● BREEDING
Sexually mature at 3–7 years; calves born singly, usually every 2–3 years; gestation lasts 10–11 months

● YOUNG
Length 76–86cm (30–33¾in) at birth, resembles adult; relies on mother's milk for 5–6 months

When the common dolphin surfaces to breathe, the sickle-shaped dorsal fin and pale markings along its flanks can be seen. Scars, known as rake marks, may also be noted.

Distribution map key

Present all year round

From the top of the head, much of the back is dark grey, brownish or purplish black or black, forming an evident 'V' shape towards the dorsal fin.

The erect dorsal fin is slender, sickle-shaped and triangular.

Tail flukes are small and neat.

Beak is well defined and dark.

The belly is pale.

Paddle-like flippers provide stability.

Waves created by a ship ploughing through the sea are often irresistible to dolphins, who can 'bow ride' for 20 minutes or more, keeping up with fast ships. They appear to relish the experience.

ANCIENT MYTHS

Myths from ancient Greece may well refer to the common dolphin. Although striped or bottle-nosed dolphins are also a possibility, the common dolphin is the most abundant in the region from which these stories originate. According to Greek myth, the sea god Poseidon was lonely without a wife and sent a dolphin messenger to call Amphitrite – one of the sea nymphs. The dolphin was so persuasive that she agreed to marry Poseidon, who in gratitude sent the dolphin to swim among the stars.

In another story, Ovid claims that *Delphinus, or Delphinius,* is the dolphin that saved the life of the 7th-century poet and musician Arion. Returning home to Greece from a tour of Sicily, Arion was seized by some sailors who planned to rob and kill him. Apparently doomed, he asked to be allowed to sing a final song. So hypnotic was the music that it attracted a group of dolphins. Seeing them, he dived into the water and one of them carried him safely home to Greece. In this tale, Apollo adds a dolphin constellation to the heavens along with the lion of Arion.

Co-operative hunting

To catch small schooling fish, common dolphins often hunt in groups. Each dolphin acts for the benefit of all, with the group working as a team to round up the fish. To concentrate their swiftly darting prey, agility and speed in the water are essential. The dolphins surround the shoal from all directions, including underneath.

Most shoaling fish respond to the presence of predators by bunching into a tight ball. They rely on the principle of safety in numbers.

The dolphins work together to corral their prey. Some members of the group remain beneath their quarry for prolonged periods.

Herds and pods

The common dolphin was named *Delphinus delphis,* or dolphin dolphin, by Swedish naturalist Carl Linnaeus in 1758. He probably thought of them as common because he saw them in large groups. In fact, the common dolphin is probably not the most abundant dolphin species, but it does sometimes form much larger herds than most others. These large herds are made up of a number of smaller herds, or pods, containing fewer than 30 dolphins, many of which are related. Around Britain and Ireland, pods usually consist of between 10 and 20 members and tend to remain separate, but sometimes up to 500 dolphins group together. Many pods have fewer than 10 animals, including pairs and singles, and these probably maintain vocal communication with other pods. The largest herds, which may number as many as 2000 or more animals, are usually found in the eastern tropical Pacific. Common dolphins socialise with other dolphin species, travelling with bottlenose, white-sided and striped dolphins – they may even mate with the latter.

Nursery groups

In the North Atlantic, common dolphins generally give birth between June and September, but little is known about when

Several members of a herd, or pod, often surface together at more or less the same moment. Their dorsal fins, located near the middle of their backs, are evident. One of the dolphins will be the leader, its movement in a particular direction followed by the rest.

◀ Usually diving for between 10 seconds and two minutes, the common dolphin must surface to breathe at least every eight minutes. Air and condensation from the lungs are explosively exhaled through the blowhole – a modified nostril – before the animal can take another quick breath.

▶ With a mighty thrust of its tail, a common dolphin catapults itself up and out of the sea. These dolphins often leap very high, possibly to increase speed – air offers less resistance than water.

this occurs in British waters. In common with many other dolphins, young adult females and nursery groups, comprising mothers and their young, separate themselves from the main herd for long periods of time. Within this group, the common dolphins are altruistic, assisting each other with birth and babysitting while a mother goes out on hunting expeditions. Females give birth to just one calf, which relies entirely on its mother for the first five to six months of life.

Swimming antics

Larger cetaceans, such as gray, fin, humpback and blue whales, create a pressure wave that common dolphins may be seen riding. The same pressure created by ocean-going ships also tempts them to ride the bow and stern waves.

While they may make use of the ride to scan for food, there is little doubt that they find it enjoyable. They are active on the surface in other ways as well. When they jump high out of the water – a manoeuvre known as breaching – they may twirl around or even somersault before landing back in the sea with a resounding splash. On occasions, they slap the water loudly with their chins, tails and flippers. A herd of dolphins is often so noisy that loud splashes can be heard from a great distance away. Even when they are below the water, their high-pitched squealing can sometimes be heard above it.

Adult common dolphins are one of the fastest animals in the sea, able to swim at very high speeds. This usually allows them to outpace their predators. Like all of the smaller cetaceans, common dolphins are fearful of killer whales – orcas – and sharks, which prey on calves as well as sick adults. If a killer whale or shark succeeds in catching a dolphin, it swallows the

Taking turns, the dolphins plunge through the centre of the ball of fish. On every foray, each one seizes more food as the others keep the fish packed together.

As the fish scatter in panic they soon become too dispersed to warrant a concerted effort. A frenzy of feeding now takes place as the dolphins engage in a free-for-all among the fish they had previously encircled.

HELP FOR STRANDED DOLPHINS

Expert help is vital if a stranded dolphin is to be saved or the cause of the stranding understood. Telephone the RSPCA on 08705 555 999 or, if in Scotland, the SSPCA (the Scottish Society for the Prevention of Cruelty to Animals) on 01313 390222. While waiting for them to arrive, keep the stranded dolphin's body wet to avoid over-heating and cover it to avoid sun or wind burn. Make sure that the blowhole is uncovered at all times. Crowds should be kept away to avoid frightening the animal even more.

If the dolphin is healthy enough to be refloated, the animal welfare officers will either wait for the tide to return, or carry the dolphin on a stretcher into the sea. Supported so that its blowhole is clear of the surface, the dolphin may be rocked to restore its circulation and ease muscle stiffness. When it can support itself and has re-orientated, the dolphin will swim off, but this often takes hours.

If the dolphin strands itself repeatedly, it is probably ill and will need treatment. Mass strandings are complicated, because dolphins that have been refloated may return to those that are still beached. In this case, sick or injured animals are removed before refloating the others. Three or four dolphins will then be refloated together, starting with those nearest the sea.

The safety of people involved in a rescue is vital, so avoid touching the animal more than necessary. Stressed dolphins can be dangerous.

Report a stranded dolphin as soon as possible. A live dolphin can survive on land for some time and, so long as some basic conditions are met, it stands a good chance of surviving.

▲ Maintaining speeds of up to 64km/h (40mph) for long periods is not unusual. The common dolphin's tapered body and complex skin structure reduce drag and help it avoid the effects of turbulence as it races along.

animal whole. Although the skin of adult dolphins is often scarred by teeth marks, these are usually caused by disputes between themselves rather than by a predator's attack.

Finding fish
All toothed cetaceans, including common dolphins, use echolocation to scan the shape of the sea bed and the coastline. They make a series of clicking noises and a special organ located in the melon-shaped bulge at the front of their heads translates the resulting echo. This guides them in their search through the murky water for schools of fish.

Common dolphins feed on a wide range of fish and squid. Around the British Isles they tend to eat flatfish on the sea bed, and small schooling fish, such as mackerel, herring and sardines, in open water. The dolphins follow the seasonal migration of their prey – in August, for instance, herring spawn off the north coast of Scotland and, in summer, sprat and sand eel, as well as mackerel, are to be found around the coasts of England and Ireland. The dolphin's long beak contains around 200 teeth – 40–55 in each side of the upper and lower jaws – for gripping on to struggling, slippery prey.

While common dolphins follow the movements of fish on which they prey, the fish in turn follow a thick band of zooplankton known as the 'scattering layer'. This drops deeper during the day to avoid sunlight and predators that forage by sight, and rises into the warmer surface waters at night.

To allow dolphins to feed at great depths, the major artery to the brain passes within the backbone, which is not the case in land mammals. This means that the dolphin's artery cannot be constricted under pressure, ensuring a constant supply of blood to the brain, even at depths of 200m (650ft) or more. Common dolphins dive regularly to depths of 50m (165ft) and, as they do not depend on sight to locate their prey, are able to feed through the night.

Hunting in packs
Schooling fish, such as sand eels and herring, are difficult for a solitary hunter to catch, so common dolphins work together to push large numbers into tight balls or drive them into narrow bays – techniques known as 'bait ball' and 'echelon' feeding.

The dolphins co-operate as a group by swimming at speed around the school of fish, slapping the surface with their tails and fins to generate a loud noise that scares the fish. They attack when the prey is tightly balled, taking it in turns to swim

◄ To court a chosen female, the male often touches the female's body gently. The male may put on a display of skill and agility by swimming directly at the female and swerving aside at the last moment.

► Subtle variations in the markings on the head and flanks of common dolphins allow experts to identify individuals. Photographic records enable the movements and behaviour of these animals to be studied throughout their lives.

through the middle, grabbing fish in their jaws. Gannets and other sea birds may take advantage of the melée by diving to seize fish from the broiling water.

Deep sea hazards

Inhabiting coastal and offshore waters means that common dolphins are affected by a wide range of different problems. Like large migratory fish, such as tuna, dolphins chase fish near the surface of the sea, leaping out of the water in pursuit of their prey. When dolphins are feeding alongside these large fish, they are often trapped in commercial nets set to catch the fish. Thousands of common dolphins have died through entanglement and

Females separate themselves from the main body of the group to give birth, sometimes in the company of other females who may act as midwives during the process. Once a new calf joins a group it can suckle from any adult female.

subsequent drowning. In European waters, common dolphins may be caught for their meat and their attraction to bow waves makes them easy targets for harpooners. Much of their prey is fished commercially, so they must search for fewer and smaller fish – another problem.

Since dolphins live in a world of sound, communicating primarily through vocalisations, any seismic explorations conducted by the oil industry and Royal Navy disturb herds off the west coast of Britain along the Atlantic seaboard.

The fact that chemical pollution is concentrated as it progresses along the food chain is another danger. The blubber and organs of dolphins tend to accumulate toxins over long periods. Many of the common dolphins that wash up on Britain's shores carry fatal burdens of contaminants. Most, however, have signs of netting on their skin, which shows that they have died in fishing nets, sometimes in groups. Others are later diagnosed with illnesses relating to a virus, toxin or parasite. Common dolphins weakened by illness show a strong drive to beach themselves to keep their blowholes above the waves. Mass strandings sometimes occur, perhaps because the leading animal is sick and so strands itself, while the other members of the social group follow it to their deaths.

Another cause of stranding is less well understood. For some reason, as yet unknown, echolocation is less effective in areas where the sea bed inclines gently towards the shore. Dolphins' specialised senses may also become confused when they follow a section of coast where the earth's magnetic field crosses the shoreline at right angles.

WILDLIFE WATCH

Where can I see common dolphins?

● One of the best places to see common dolphins is around the Isle of Mull in the Hebrides – boat trips are available with guides from the Hebridean Whale and Dolphin Trust. If watching from the mainland, try Strumble Head, Pembrokeshire.

● Dolphins occur in coastal waters around Cornwall, north-west Scotland and County Cork in Ireland. Along the west coast of Britain, July–October is the best time to see them, although they may be there all year.

● From a boat near the Hebrides, or to the west of Ireland, there's a chance of seeing large groups near the edge of the continental shelf.

● Dolphins do not survive long in captivity, so they are rarely kept in aquariums.

● For more information, telephone the Sea Watch Foundation on 01865 717276, or the Hebridean Whale and Dolphin Trust on 01688 302620.

The herring gull

Broad, powerful wings enable this large bird to skim the waves and snatch fish from just below the surface. Flocks congregate in fishing harbours and on reservoirs in winter, when food is scarce. Some may even scavenge inland in towns and cities.

In most seaside towns the raucous voice of the herring gull is a familiar sound. This large bird is also a common sight, soaring over the sea, perching on roofs, ledges and railings or walking along piers and jetties. It may swoop low over the heads of humans, although it rarely makes contact, swerving upwards at the last minute, perhaps uttering its high-pitched, wailing call.

Today, the herring gull is one of Britain's most ubiquitous sea birds. The secret of its success lies in its versatility. It is a predator, scavenger and food pirate, and its varied diet means that it will take any food item of suitable size and texture for swallowing.

Winter scavenging

Although plenty of food is available on the coast, herring gulls are attracted to easy pickings inland. This is particularly true in winter, when some of their sea prey becomes scarcer. Then herring gulls are frequently encountered in urban areas, lured by the size and number of rubbish tips found around most cities. In some areas, crowds of herring gulls attracted to rubbish dumps and landfill sites have become a cause for concern. It is thought they may sometimes spread diseases such as gastroenteritis. However, herring gulls present no real threat to human health unless they gather in large numbers on waters supplying reservoirs.

Not just a scavenger, the herring gull is also an accomplished fisher, using its strong, sharply hooked bill to seize its prey. A hunting herring gull may dip on to the surface, or even plunge into the water if the prey warrants the effort.

As these opportunistic birds hop and walk among the refuse, picking it over with their powerful bills, they have been known to eat some unusual items, including bonfire charcoal, matchboxes, rope, greaseproof paper and the rubber seals around car sun-roofs.

In towns and cities, herring gulls also congregate outside fast-food shops, rip open bin liners and pull rubbish from dustbins awaiting collection.

HERRING GULL FACT FILE

One of Britain's largest gulls, the herring gull is a stocky, thick-necked bird with a strongly hooked, deep yellow bill and pinkish legs. Winter visitors from Scandinavia are distinguished by their darker grey upperparts and by having less black on their wing tips.

● **NAMES**
Common name: herring gull
Scientific name: *Larus argentatus*

● **HABITAT**
Open, sloping ground, cliff ledges and tops of buildings, especially near ports and harbours; refuse sites, lakes, sewage works and agricultural land; moorland

● **DISTRIBUTION**
All round coastline and increasingly inland; found in greatest numbers in north and west

● **STATUS**
Most numerous British gull; about 144,000 pairs breed in Britain and about 45,000 pairs in Ireland; probably 500,000 individuals present in winter, when population is increased by immigrants from north-western Europe

● **SIZE**
Length 55–67cm (22–26in); wingspan 123–148cm (48–58in); weight 750–1450g (26–51oz)

● **KEY FEATURES**
Heavy body with long, broad, tapering wings; back and wings silvery to bluish grey; white underparts; head white, becoming streaked with brownish grey in winter; stout, hook-tipped bill with orange-red spot; juvenile mottled grey-brown with dark wing tips and tail band and blackish bill

● **HABITS**
Nests in colonies; scavenges rubbish tips; follows ploughs and fishing boats; bullies other sea birds; cannibalistic

● **VOICE**
Mainly wailing, yelping or laughing, short barks and deep 'kyou-kyou-kyou'; soft, nervous 'ga-ga-ga' of alarm; long call is a loud, clear 'au-kyoo kau-kau-kau-kau-kau-kau-kau-kau-kau'

● **FOOD**
Crustaceans and fish plus fruits, seeds, vegetables, invertebrates, small mammals, sea birds, their chicks and eggs, carrion, offal, food scraps

● **BREEDING**
Eggs laid mid-April–June; single brood per season

● **NEST**
A sizeable mound of vegetation, lined with finer material; sited on open ground, cliff ledges and buildings (mainly roofs)

● **EGGS**
2–4, usually 3, pale olive or yellowy brown with dark grey or blackish brown markings; incubated by both parents for about 4 weeks

● **YOUNG**
Downy grey with darker markings; hatch separately with 1–2 days between chicks; leave nest after 2–3 days but remain close by and fledge at 5–6 weeks

Although the herring gull's nest is seldom left unattended by the adult birds, both eggs and young are sufficiently well camouflaged to avoid detection by any passing predators, such as foxes, hedgehogs, rats and birds, including crows, magpies and other large gulls.

The yellow beak has an orange-red spot near its whitish tip.

A narrow, fleshy, deep yellow or orange ring surrounds the eye, which has a pale lemon yellow iris.

Both the back and wings are silver to bluish grey.

Wing tips are black with white spots, known as 'mirrors'.

Breast and underparts are white.

Short and robust, the legs are pink or pinkish grey.

Distribution map key

■ Present all year round

■ Present during winter months

□ Not present

▲ The herring gull is among the most significant predators of tern chicks. Some tern colonies have been wiped out by attacks from large gulls, including the herring gull.

◄ A dead fish discarded by an angler or trawler is likely to be quickly seized by a herring gull. Any herring gull that grabs a fish seldom has the chance to consume it without first having to fight off at least one other competitor.

Feeding tactics

As well as urban areas, farmland provides good feeding opportunities for herring gulls, and they often follow tractors in search of earthworms and insect larvae exposed by the plough. For the best part of the year, however, they catch most of their prey from around the coast – fish from the sea and, on land and in the shallows, small mammals and the young of other birds.

Another feeding tactic is to capture live prey, such as a hard-shelled crab or mollusc, then carry it up into the air and drop it from a great height on to a hard surface. This skill requires a period of learning for young herring gulls before they are able to execute it efficiently.

Young birds often drop the prey over water at first, but their technique improves gradually as they mature. In north-western Europe herring gulls regularly capture frogs emerging from cracks in the ice on frozen lakes, carry them to a height of 10–15m (33–50ft), then drop them on to the ice. This is repeated up to four times, until the frog is battered and becomes easy for the herring gull to swallow.

Although herring gulls are large, they are deft and agile in flight, and quick to spot potential food. They can usually outpace slower rivals with ease in order to grab the choicest morsels. If competitors do get there first, herring gulls are liable to use their size to intimidate the birds,

including other gulls, wrestling food from them or stealing it from under their beaks. Herring gulls will harry other sea birds, such as auks, into relinquishing prey that they have caught for their offspring, and even kill small migrating birds over the sea.

Roosting on roofs

A few decades ago, when the herring gull population increased, some colonies expanded so much that the birds developed the habit of taking up residence on the roofs of houses. For the human occupants this means being kept awake by the gulls' squabbling and woken early by a raucous reveille from the gulls' very loud wailing and laughing calls.

Raiding fishing boats

Although its relative, the lesser black-backed gull, often follows fishing trawlers far out to sea in summer, the herring gull waits closer to shore – usually within sight of land – until the boats return to harbour. While the fishermen sort the catch, the gulls snatch a meal.

A gull notices a small item of food carried to the surface by the swell created by the boat's propellers, and settles on the water to investigate.

As the gull takes to the air, it must keep a watchful eye open for other birds that will soon try to steal from it.

Herring gulls are quick to spot a fishing boat returning to port. They follow in its wake, waiting for dead fish to fall or be thrown overboard.

HERRING GULL CALENDAR

January • February

Herring gulls, including juveniles such as this one, live wherever they can find food, on the coast and inland, but from mid-February onwards, each herring gull starts to spend more time at its coastal breeding colony.

March • April

By mid-March, pairs have re-formed and single birds find mates at 'clubs'. Pairs build a bulky nest and the female lays the first eggs in mid-April. Both parents participate in incubating the eggs, taking turns.

May • June

Four weeks later, the eggs hatch. The adults learn to recognise their own chicks in the first few days after hatching, and will attack those of other pairs. The downy young fledge at five to six weeks.

July • August

The summer months are a challenging period for young herring gulls. Once their parents have severed ties, they are forced to scavenge for themselves along the seashore. They have not yet learnt all the feeding skills of adults.

September • October

Herring gull breeding colonies start to break up in September as the birds disperse in search of food. Migrant herring gulls from Europe arrive, joining resident birds on the coast and at inland freshwater sites.

November • December

Most birds spend the winter on the coast, where they gather at places where food is readily available, such as ports. Large congregations of herring gulls are also found at inland sites, such as reservoirs and rubbish dumps.

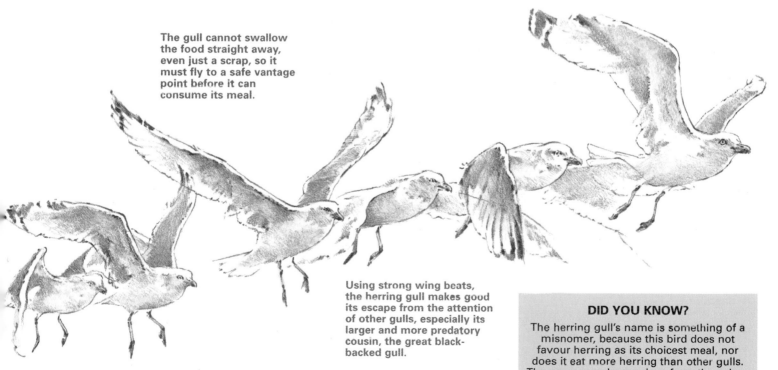

The gull cannot swallow the food straight away, even just a scrap, so it must fly to a safe vantage point before it can consume its meal.

Using strong wing beats, the herring gull makes good its escape from the attention of other gulls, especially its larger and more predatory cousin, the great black-backed gull.

DID YOU KNOW?

The herring gull's name is something of a misnomer, because this bird does not favour herring as its choicest meal, nor does it eat more herring than other gulls. The name may have arisen from the colour of the bird's back and wings, which are silvery, resembling the colour of herring.

BEGGING CHICKS

When an adult herring gull returns to its nest with food, its chicks scurry out of their hiding places to peck at the red spot on its beak. This spot is called a 'social releaser' by scientists, because it prompts – or releases – the begging instinct of the chicks. The adult responds by regurgitating food on to the ground and then offering titbits to each of its hungry offspring. As the chicks grow older, they replace this bill-pecking begging behaviour with neck-pumping and crying, sometimes calling up to 60 times per minute for food.

▲ Seen close-up, the herring gull has a yellow eye and a well-marked bill with an orange-red spot that is a conspicuous signal to its chicks.

◄ Herring gull chicks elicit food from their parents by begging repetitively. The begging behaviour takes different forms as the chicks mature.

Given the size of an adult herring gull, it is perhaps not surprising that mating is a rough and tumble affair. Mating usually takes place in the vicinity of the nest site, on the ground or on a favoured perch.

Another aspect of the herring gull's use of roofs is that passers-by, walking beneath the birds' nests, risk being dive-bombed by droppings. This choice of location may be unpopular with humans, but it gives herring gulls a plentiful supply of suitable nest sites. Nests are built in the same way as those on cliff ledges, comprising a large mound of vegetation.

Noisy colonies

Away from the roofs of houses, the traditional breeding sites of herring gulls include coastal cliffs, dunes, shingle beaches, reservoirs and large lakes. Both members of a pair defend their chosen territory, which is made up of the nest and a vantage point where the adults perch. A safe area behind the vantage point is first used for courtship and mating, then for nest building, rearing the chicks and resting.

Even colonies that are large and loose, with plenty of nest sites available, can be noisy places. Squabbles break out over favoured places to perch. The gulls glare at their rivals, stretching upwards then bowing forwards, pecking the ground and plucking at the grass or some other nearby object in a threatening manner. Any creature that attempts a raid on a herring gull nest is treated to a similar display. One look at the adult's powerfully hooked bill is usually enough to deter most would-be predators.

Forming pairs

Herring gulls usually breed for the first time when they are between four and six years old, although they may be aged from three to seven. They are generally monogamous but pairs do sometimes separate for reasons unknown. The birds start to gather in their breeding colonies in February, either singly or in pairs. Single gulls may meet potential mates at daytime roosts, or 'clubs', which are made up of other non-breeders and juveniles.

At the start of each season, the pair bond is re-established with courtship rituals and feeding. This behaviour is most intense 10 days before laying, then the birds settle down to their incubation duties. The chicks hatch after around 28 days. They leave the nest soon after, but remain within their parents' territory until they take their first flights at five to

Of all birds, the herring gull is one of the most regular visitors to rubbish tips. Its powerful, hook-tipped bill allows it to tear open even the strongest bin liners to investigate their contents.

▲ As with all other birds, feather care is of vital importance to the herring gull. Bathing – in a freshwater lake or reservoir if possible – along with preening occupy an hour or more of their time each day.

On house roofs structural features such as chimneys offer herring gulls a secure framework around which to build their nests. Here, the birds are in a safe, raised position, as in their more traditional clifftop sites, and food is available nearby.

six weeks. The few youngsters that inadvertently stray from the nest area are quite often killed by neighbouring gulls.

Stealing chicks

Initially, the chicks are in danger from their own parents, because for the first five days after hatching the adults are not able to distinguish their own young from those of other herring gulls. As they grow and become bolder, the chicks roam more widely. On hearing an alarm call from its parents, however, a chick will return promptly to its favoured hiding place. Parents stand guard over their offspring day and night for the first two to three weeks, but thereafter they are left alone while the adults feed.

While they are away, neighbouring gulls may sneak into the nest site and steal one of the chicks. In larger broods, a single chick is unlikely to be missed. Although the thief intends to take the youngster back to its own nest to eat, it often adopts it instead. When the chick starts begging for food, the adult's parental instincts override its cannibalistic urges. It seems returning to the familiar surroundings of its own nest and young influences the bird's behaviour. A chick may even have several foster parents on adjacent territories and be fed by any of them.

Changing population

From the 1940s to the late 1960s, the herring gull population increased dramatically, probably due to the greater availability of food in urban areas in winter. However, by the late 1980s, numbers had almost halved due to local culling, improved refuse disposal, being taken by foxes and botulism – to which gulls are particularly susceptible.

A herring gull is often very adventurous in what it eats. It will attempt to consume the unlikeliest of meals, such as this starfish, especially during the winter when food becomes scarce.

The gannet

This large, gleaming white sea bird breeds on remote rocky coasts and islands. Although many gannets fly south for the winter, some have already returned to their colonies by late December.

Although the gannet – or northern gannet as it is officially known – has suffered breeding failures in recent years, it is now increasing in those parts of the British Isles where there is an abundance of food. The small fish upon which gannets feed, such as herring, have increased in numbers because fishermen catch so many of the bigger fish that prey on them. Unwanted fish thrown back into the sea from trawlers provide another major supply of food.

Between 1968 and 1970, Britain and Ireland had just under 140,000 pairs of gannets, but now that figure has risen to more than half as much again. British and Irish gannets represent about two-thirds of the world population. Not only have birds in established colonies, or gannetries, bred successfully, but gannets have formed new breeding colonies.

Traditional colonies may not be able to expand far because not enough suitable land or ledges are available in the immediate vicinity for the increasing number of birds to occupy. Also, areas where more fish have appeared may be too far away for birds from established sites to reach easily. This produces a pattern of new colonies being set up quite a long way from existing ones, located near the new fishing grounds.

Gannets' breeding colonies are crowded, noisy places, where there is much competition for space, even though each bird returns to the same nest, and the same mate, each year.

These new gannetries often become established and develop fairly quickly. They grow at different rates but generally much faster than would be possible if fuelled by breeding alone. It seems likely, therefore, that the plentiful supply of food lures an influx of birds to desert traditional colonies each year and transfer to the fresh locations, where fish populations are thriving.

GANNET FACT FILE

Thanks to its long body and wings, the gannet is larger than any other sea bird that breeds in the North Atlantic. Its flight is distinctive, with fast, shallow wingbeats alternating with brief glides.

● NAMES
Common names: gannet, northern gannet, solan goose; young known as guga
Scientific name: *Morus bassanus* (previously *Sula bassana*)

● DISTRIBUTION
23 colonies around British and Irish coasts and offshore islands, including two on Alderney in the Channel Islands

● STATUS
Around 227,000 pairs in Britain and 33,000 pairs in Ireland

● SIZE
Length 87–100cm (34¼–40in); wingspan 170–192cm (67–76¾in); weight 2.4–3.6kg (5–8lb)

● KEY FEATURES
Large size, white and black plumage with black wing tips; buff-yellow wash on back of head; bill dagger-shaped, pale blue-grey, marked with black lines, almost 10cm (4in) long; legs dark, blue lines on feet; pointed tail

● HABITS
Gathers in large numbers when plunge diving; birds may swim on surface; nests in colonies

● VOICE
Feeding groups may utter various harsh calls; at colony, gives loud, harsh barks, croaks and groans, especially deep rasping *'urrah-urrah'* call, producing a mechanical-sounding rhythmic chorus; young have yapping calls

● FOOD
Small fish up to 20–30cm (8–12in), including herring, sprat, mackerel, pilchard and sand eel; also fish and fish offal discarded from trawlers

● BREEDING
Earliest birds return to colony late December; some adults still on nests in early November; egg laid late April–May; young fledge in late August–September

● NEST
Large, compacted pile of seaweed, grass, earth and feathers, cemented with excreta; pair return to same nest each year, adding to it annually, the male doing most of the work; nests sited close together on cliff edges, steep slopes and flatter ground, evenly spaced out

● EGGS
Single egg, pale, translucent blue turning white, covered in chalky layer, stained during incubation; male and female take turns with the egg, each turn averaging more than a day; incubating birds stand on egg, wrapping the warm webs of their feet over it; chick hatches after 6 weeks, typically 44 days

● YOUNG
Same as adult, but plumage brown speckled with white; brooded on parents' webbed feet continuously for first 14 days; independent on fledging at around 13 weeks

Distribution map key

■	Present all year round
■	Breeding colonies
□	Not present

In strong winds, the gannet soars and glides effortlessly on stiffly held, pointed wings. These are tipped with black and have an angular appearance when in flight.

Mainly snow white plumage shows up the buff-yellow colouring on the back of the head.

With a broad base, the bill is long and pointed.

The body is long and cigar-shaped.

Both webbed feet have pale blue lines along the toes.

When it spots a shoal of fish, the gannet circles slowly before beginning its descent.

Using its large feet like rudders in the air gives the gannet more control over its direction.

The gannet selects a target and increases its speed by drawing back its long wings, which span around 1.8m (6ft).

During the dive the bird can extend its approach by moving its wings forward.

Drawing the wings towards the body increases the speed further until...

Plunge dive

The gannet flies over the sea in search of shoals of fish. When it sees potential prey, the bird plunges down to snatch fish a few metres, or feet, below the surface. As it dives, it uses its long wings and streamlined body to build speed, and its large feet to manoeuvre itself accurately towards its target.

GANNET CALENDAR

JANUARY ● FEBRUARY

Most adults return to the colonies early in the year to claim their nesting site. Some birds remain farther south, and many young birds are still at sea off West Africa or in the Mediterranean.

MARCH ● APRIL

Adult birds that will breed have mostly returned to the colonies, where they squabble over nest sites and steal nest material from each other, while cementing their pair bonds.

MAY ● JUNE

The female lays a single egg, usually in late April or early May. Most eggs hatch in June. Birds may feed quite a distance away from the colonies and non-breeders roam farther afield.

JULY ● AUGUST

As the chicks grow, they demand food hungrily. Streams of adults shuttle to and fro between the colony and the feeding grounds, bringing regular meals back to the growing chicks.

SEPTEMBER ● OCTOBER

Most of the white-speckled dark brown young leave the colonies in September to disperse southwards. However, many adults and immature birds from previous years remain at the colonies.

NOVEMBER ● DECEMBER

Outside the breeding season almost all gannets are at sea, unperturbed by even very stormy weather. A few birds may remain at the colonies until early November.

An indication of the gannet's success is that while there were just nine colonies in the British Isles in 1900, today there are 23. Those at Foula and Fair Isle in Shetland, Troup Head in Grampian, Clare Island in County Mayo and Ireland's Eye off Dublin have been established for 30 years or so. In 2003 two very small ones were started in Orkney. Three others – Great Saltee off County Wexford, Scar Rocks in Wigtown Bay in Dumfries and Galloway, and Bempton in Yorkshire – were formed between 1929 and 1939.

A pair of gannets raises just one chick each year. A gannet's egg is quite small in relation to the adult bird's size so that a female would be capable of producing two within a few days of each other. That the birds never lay two eggs suggests a larger family has not been an option in their evolutionary history.

Two relatives of the gannet, the cormorant and the shag, lay more eggs. The cormorant usually lays three or four and the shag mostly three but up to six.

...with only a short distance to go, the gannet, eyes fixed on its target, tucks wings, legs and tail together.

These birds start breeding at a younger age than the four to six years typical of the gannet. Gannets, however, are much better at surviving and the oldest recorded individual in the British Isles was 37 years and four months old. This is a good deal longer than the maximum age for cormorants and shags.

Communal feeding

The gannet's feeding technique is an amazing spectacle. A foraging bird cruises over a wide area of sea. When it spots a shoal of fish swimming just below the surface, it circles and dives into the water. Its white, flashing wings are easily observed from afar by other birds. They congregate quickly at the site to feed on the shoaling fish.

This apparently altruistic behaviour of signalling the location of prey to others means that the bird will have to share the pickings. A large flock of gannets will soon decimate a shoal, if they do not scare the fish into retreating to safer depths. However, gannets have good reason to inform others when they discover prey. By itself, an individual gannet will come across a decent shoal of fish just once in a while, but it will benefit from the discoveries of other birds time after time.

The gannet makes use of updraughts of air around the cliffs at its breeding site to help it manoeuvre when taking off and landing. In the melée around a colony, a gannet will sometimes hang motionless in the air on a strong updraught before landing.

When hunting, the birds all fly in the same direction – into the wind – to reduce their speed across the water. They generally cruise at about 10–12m (33–39ft), but sometimes up to 30–50m (100–165ft) above the surface. Most dives are not vertical, but involve an adjustment of angle or body position. With wings swept back, their beaks pierce the sea at speeds that sometimes exceed 100km/h (62mph). As the gannets hit the water, they may throw up a jet of spray visible for up to several kilometres.

As the gannet plunges into the sea, it forms such a streamlined shape that the water offers little resistance.

Fish sometimes form large shoals close to the surface of the sea, making them an easy target for these skilful fishing birds. Deeper shoals require greater flight speeds, in which case the gannet may start its dive when 30m (100ft) or more above the waves.

Squabbling over food

Where many gannets have congregated to fish together, they may attempt to ambush each other and steal fish. A gannet with a fish in its bill must get it quickly into a position where it may be swallowed in one gulp.

When there is competition from other birds, the gannet manipulates its catch in its bill while splashing to keep away potential thieves.

Gannets have specially constructed skulls, modified to help absorb the shock of impact with water. Their bills, unlike those of most other birds, have no external nostrils so that water is not forced into them – the bird breathes through its mouth and holds its breath underwater. Air sacs under the skin of the face and chest act like bubble-wrap to cushion those parts that hit the water. Gannets have eyes that are sited relatively far forwards on the face, giving them excellent vision for accurate judgement of distance.

Feeding frenzy

Often feeding appears to be a disorganised frenzy of activity, with dozens, even hundreds, of birds plunging repeatedly into the water from a great height. Each bird must not only make sure that it does not collide with other birds, but also search the waters below for fish. The birds typically plunge about 3m (10ft) into the water, rarely reaching more than 4.5m (15ft) deep through the force of the dive, although they may swim down as far as 15m (40ft), using powerful strokes of their wings and webbed feet. They often chase fish and usually swallow their prey underwater unless it is very big.

The male brings offerings of seaweed with which to line the nest. Some males may simply gather such material from the vicinity of the nest or even steal it from the nests of unwary neighbours.

COMMUNICATING PAIRS

Fairly unusually in the bird world, gannets form monogamous pairs for life. The birds look for nest sites from their third year onwards and begin breeding from between four and six years old. The pair bond is renewed each year and, having spent the winter months separately, the couple greet each other ceremonially by conspicuous and prolonged 'fencing' with their bills. They also clatter their bills together and call raucously, making the ritual a very noisy affair.

When one member of the pair contemplates going off to forage, it warns its mate of its intention. Otherwise, should they both decide to depart at the same time, their precious egg or chick could be left defenceless among their neighbours. The bird indicates its intention to leave the colony by a behaviour known as sky pointing. This involves standing in a position in which its beak points directly upwards at the sky. Lifting its feet slowly in an exaggerated manner, on the spot, while gazing determinedly forwards, reinforces the bird's message.

Should the other member of the pair also wish to leave the colony at this time, the two birds display to one another until eventually one individual backs down and becomes less intense in its display. Then the successful bird runs, jumps or launches itself into the air. As it does so, it utters an unusual cry that sounds like a soft groan.

◄ Greeting partners stand close together, breast to breast, holding their wings outstretched and shaking and ducking their heads, often snaking their necks over the back and neck of their mate.

► Signalling to a partner by 'sky pointing' entails the bird standing with its head and neck stretched upwards so that its beak points at the sky. The bird also raises its wing tips and lets its tail drop.

▲ In the gannetries, territories are established around each nest by the distance that a bird can stab with its bill. The formidable, spear-like bills can be used to inflict a lot of damage, quite often drawing blood. Both males and females are aggressive but the males particularly so.

▼ For 12 weeks one or other parent is rarely absent from their single chick. They alternate between foraging and brooding duties, and each brings one or two feeds a day. On a diet of regurgitated fish the chick fattens up swiftly and, before fledging, becomes heavier than its parents.

While flocks of feeding birds are conspicuous and soon attract more and more gannets to share the food, there is usually plenty for all. Fishermen even use sightings of groups of gannets to flag up places where fish are shoaling. If the shoal swims too deep for the birds to be able to catch them, the feeding frenzy can stop as quickly as it started

On occasions, gannets can become a nuisance to fishermen who are hauling in their nets. The birds are aware of the fishing boats in the area and seem to recognise the change in sounds coming from a boat that is starting to winch its nets aboard. The gannets often attempt to steal fish as they are hauled from the sea. However, the concentration of fish in a successful haul can cause excited birds to get caught in the netting and even to dive fatally on to the deck.

Gannets also follow trawlers from which undersized fish or offal are being discarded. Swimming on the surface, they pick up discards as soon as they are thrown over the side, or dive from the surface to retrieve them in the manner of a cormorant or shag.

Busy nesting sites

Each pair returns to the same nest every year. Adults will sometimes defend the nest site for 10–11 months of the year because, in large and growing colonies, there is intense competition for space. This results in fighting, accompanied by harsh, excited cries. The birds engage in wrestling matches, gripping each other's beak or face in an attempt to push a rival off the site. Disagreement may continue in the air or on the sea. However, most of the time

aggression is avoided through a ritualised bowing display that signals ownership of a particular site and functions as a threat to repel intruders. Nests are spaced at a distance of about 70cm (28in) from centre to centre – the sparring distance of the owners – so that neighbours cannot quite reach each other and are safe where they are.

Along with seaweed, gannets often bring back fish netting to line their nests, but the use of modern materials that do not rot means that both adults and young risk becoming entangled in the mesh. At several accessible colonies, conservationists remove the dangerous material in the winter during the short time when the birds are absent.

Young gannets are a dark greyish brown with a spangling of white tips to the feathers. Gradually, over four years or so,

the white adult plumage develops and the birds look blotchy. The last feathers to be lost are usually the secondary wing feathers – the long feathers on the rear half of the inner wings. Blotchy birds can be aged quite accurately in flight. Brown birds finely speckled with white are sometimes seen flying south from the colonies, although some birds with traces of brown feathers occupy nesting sites.

WILDLIFE WATCH

Where can I see gannets?

● Gannets can be seen off almost any coast in the British Isles for most of the year. Binoculars are essential, except possibly from headlands. In bright weather, distant flashes of gleaming white birds with long, narrow wings are most likely to be gannets.

● Colonies are often in such remote areas that visits are out of the question. On islands, where the birds are not used to visitors landing and coming close, serious losses can result. However, there are several colonies where the birds can be observed, some of which are listed below.

● Bass rock, Firth of Forth, not far east of Edinburgh, is an island less than 3km (2 miles) offshore that supports a large and historic colony of slightly more than 48,000 breeding pairs. Constant streams of adults flying to and from the colony can be seen from the coast east of North Berwick. Small boats are licensed to take visitors around the island and some are permitted to land.

● Bempton cliffs on the north side of Flamborough Head in east Yorkshire has an RSPB car park and visitor centre. Clifftop paths give good views of the only English gannet colony, which was founded about 75 years ago. It now supports more than 2500 breeding pairs.

● Hermaness, on Unst in the Shetland Isles, houses more than 100,000 pairs of various sea birds, of which more than 12,000 are pairs of gannets. They breed in colonies on the northern cliffs overlooking Muckle Flugga. The site is reached by parking at the end of the B9086 road and walking the path to the clifftop.

● The tiny Welsh island of Grassholm, off Pembrokeshire, has more than 32,400 pairs of gannets, covering about a third of the northern part of the island. Circumnavigation can be arranged by taking a small boat from Martinshaven, among other harbours. Crossings are available from 15 June onwards and should be booked in advance.

Recognising coastal waders

When the wind is cold and the hours of daylight limited, vast numbers of wading birds flock to seashores and estuaries, providing a spectacle eye-catching enough to brighten up the bleakest day.

Winter flocks of knot can run into thousands. Swirling clouds of birds take to the air when they are disturbed from their roosts on remote estuaries.

Trying to identify, at a glance, many of the species of waders that crowd the British coast in winter can be difficult. Some, such as the oystercatcher, are unmistakable, but after the breeding season is over many waders moult into a rather nondescript winter plumage of greyish brown and white, losing many of their most conspicuous features. Then, it is necessary to look for more subtle plumage differences between similar species, or distinctions of form, such as

the different leg lengths of the two species of godwit. Often the best clues are supplied by the bird's activities – a small, very pale, dark-billed wader racing along the surf line on a sandy beach like a clockwork toy can be confidently identified as a sanderling, even if the details of its plumage are not visible, because no other wader shares this habit. A much darker, stockier bird, streaked beneath, feeding on an exposed rocky promontory near the tide line is likely to be

a purple sandpiper. A curlew tends to forage rather slowly and deliberately, while the similar but smaller whimbrel is often more active and agile.

Peak season

It is worth mastering the problems of recognising these birds in winter plumage, because this is one of the peak seasons for coastal waders. Adult birds, together with potentially confusing juveniles fledged earlier in the year, arrive in huge numbers from their northern breeding

grounds in autumn, and many remain throughout the winter. Some species, such as knots, form immense flocks on broad estuaries, which are among the most impressive wildlife spectacles in Europe. Indeed, the bays and estuaries of the British coastline are internationally important refuges for many of these birds. For other species, the coasts of Britain and Ireland are just staging posts on a long journey that will take them to the Mediterranean or Africa, but they can often be seen at either end of the season. Most of the scarcer species turn up in autumn, particularly juvenile birds that have probably strayed off-course through lack of navigation experience.

Feeding adaptations

Waders are an extremely diverse group of birds with a wide range of special adaptations. Some of these differences may not be immediately apparent, but since many waders feed in mixed flocks in the open on marshes and estuaries during the winter, the season offers an ideal opportunity to compare the different species.

Legs and feet

Most of the special feeding adaptations that have evolved among closely related species have arisen because of the need to minimise competition, and exploit every available feeding opportunity. Among waders, foraging techniques are largely governed by the leg length and bill structure of each species.

Not surprisingly, the longer a wader's legs, the deeper the water that it tends to feed in. So the curlew, whimbrel, avocet, and two species of godwit regularly wade in water that is more than 15cm (6in) deep, while shorter redshanks are confined to the shallows. Short-legged species, such as knots and dunlins, tend to stay out of the water altogether, feeding on wet sand or mud, but dunlins will wade quite deeply on occasion, showing that the rule is not infallible.

The feet of waders have three spreading, forward-facing toes and a reduced hind toe. The broad spread

One of the few waders that is instantly identifiable in winter, the avocet has brilliant white and jet black plumage, and a uniquely upcurved bill. This adult is taking a vigorous bath.

of the three main toes distributes the weight of the bird, enabling it to walk on soft, waterlogged mud and sand without sinking. Interestingly, an avocet has slight webbing between its front toes, an adaptation that enables it to feed even when the ground on which it is walking is extremely muddy. It also allows the bird to swim when crossing deeper channels – something that most waders avoid.

Specialised bills

Waders are best known for the variety of their bills. The most robust tool is the long, stout carrot-coloured bill of the oystercatcher, which the bird uses to chisel open the tough shells of bivalve molluscs, such as mussels, and hammer limpets from rocks. By contrast, the redshank uses its long, but

less sturdy, bill to pick tiny molluscs from the estuary mud, or probe a little way beneath the surface for small crustaceans and other burrowing invertebrates, such as marine worms.

The turnstone lives up to its name by employing its short, stout bill to flip over stones and seaweed on rocky shores and sheltered beaches, revealing small animals which it then seizes before they can escape. At the other extreme, the curlew uses its extraordinarily long, downcurved bill to delve deeply into mud and sand to extract marine worms and crabs from their burrows, probing deeper than any other wader. Bar-tailed and black-tailed godwits use their long, straight bills to extract worms and molluscs in a similar way, but since they cannot reach quite as deep

as the curlew, they avoid competing for exactly the same food.

The greenshank favours a stabbing or side-to-side sweeping action of its slightly upcurved bill, wading in deeper water where its prey includes shrimps and small fish taken from the water itself. The bill of the elegant avocet is upcurved to a much greater degree to suit a similar but more specialised feeding technique, which involves the bird sweeping its bill from side to side in the shallows and oozing mud to harvest small creatures concealed by the turbid water.

WILDLIFE WATCH

Where can I see coastal waders?

● A visit to an estuary in winter is almost certain to be rewarded by views of the waders that spend the colder months on British and Irish coasts. The largest numbers are to be found on the more well-known sites, such as Snettisham RSPB Reserve on Norfolk's Wash, where tens of thousands of knots come to roost at high tide. Any estuary with tidal mudflats is worth exploring.

● Before making the trip, check the tides. Try to visit the coast at a time when the tide is rising, as it will push the birds closer to the shore. At low tide, waders feeding in large estuaries and bays may be too far away to see clearly, even with a telescope.

● Larger waders such as curlews, godwits, redshanks and greenshanks are common on most estuaries in winter.

● Small numbers of turnstones occur on most beaches around the British Isles from September to March. They feed among rocks and seaweed but also along the strand line. Sanderlings and purple sandpipers can be seen in the same months.

● Spotted redshank can be seen on north Kent and Essex estuaries, the Hampshire coast and in south-west Wales. The prime wintering site for avocets is the Exe estuary in Devon.

EASY GUIDE TO SPOTTING COASTAL WADERS

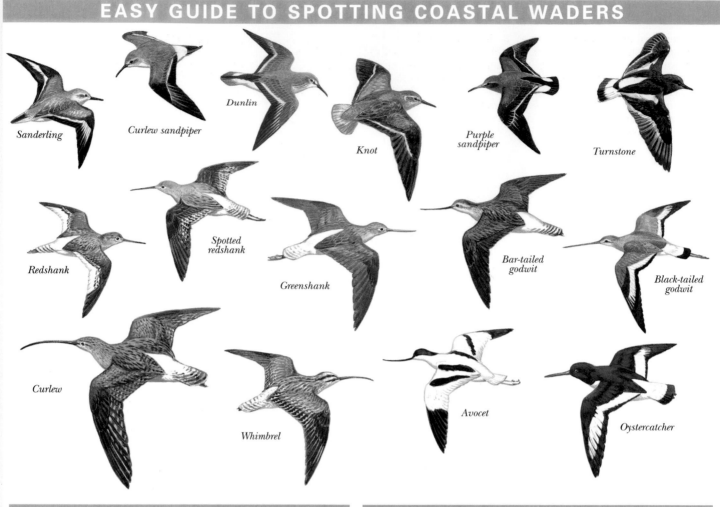

Sanderling

Curlew sandpiper

Dunlin

Knot

Purple sandpiper

Turnstone

Redshank

Spotted redshank

Greenshank

Bar-tailed godwit

Black-tailed godwit

Curlew

Whimbrel

Avocet

Oystercatcher

WHAT ARE COASTAL WADERS?

● All waders belong to the order Charadriiformes, a large and diverse group of mainly oceanic and shore birds that includes gulls, skuas, terns and auks, as well as waders.

● Within the Charadriiformes, the oystercatcher is the only British species that belongs to the family Haematopodidae.

● The avocet belongs to the family Recurvirostridae, which includes stilts as well as other species of avocet that are not seen in Britain.

● The knot, sanderling, dunlin, turnstone, sandpipers, godwits, curlew, whimbrel and various species of 'shanks' belong to the family Scolopacidae. This group also includes snipes – waders that are found mainly on freshwater wetlands rather than coasts.

● Other coastal waders include plovers, which belong to the family Charadriidae.

● Almost all waders spend the winter feeding in water or wet mud or sand, either on coasts and estuaries, or on freshwater marshes. As a consequence, many show adaptations for walking in water and probing, such as long legs and long bills.

● In spring, most species of waders migrate to moorland or Arctic tundra to breed. Here they may feed largely on the insects that breed in freshwater bog and tundra pools. So these species are 'coastal' in winter only.

● Despite this, some waders can be seen in small numbers throughout the year at estuaries and other coastal sites. These birds include non-breeders, passage migrants and species that nest on nearby wetlands.

Distribution map key

■ Present all year round

□ Present during summer months

■ Present during winter months

■ Present during breeding season

□ Spring and autumn passage migrant

□ Not present

HOW CAN I IDENTIFY COASTAL WADERS?

● The sanderling is the only small, pale grey and white wader likely to be seen running along a sandy beach by the breakers.

● The dunlin is the most common small wader – a rounded bird with a longish, tapered, slightly curved black bill.

● Purple and curlew sandpipers are similar to dunlin. The former can be recognised by its mustard-yellow legs, the latter by its bold white rump, visible in flight.

● Knots are medium-sized waders with white wingbars, dumpy bodies and grey-green legs. They often occur in flocks of thousands.

● The turnstone's stocky shape is a clue to its identity, as is its habit of turning over stones to feed. In winter, its chestnut and black upperparts turn a dull blackish brown.

● The redshank is easily recognised by its red legs, long red-based bill, loud call and white trailing edge on its inner wing. The spotted redshank is similar, but has more elegant proportions and a different call. Also, it lacks white on its upper wings.

● Greenshanks have clean, pale-looking plumage and bluish green legs. The bill is longer and more robust than the redshank's, and is slightly upturned.

● Both species of godwit look superficially similar, but the bar-tailed godwit has narrow bars on its tail, whereas the black-tailed has a broad black band. They are easiest to distinguish in flight, when only the black-tailed godwit shows striking white wingbars.

● The curlew and whimbrel are similar in appearance, although the curlew is larger, paler, and has longer legs. A whimbrel has distinctive head stripes and a bill that curves down more abruptly near the end. The curlew calls its name, while the common call of the whimbrel is a descending series of whistles.

● Avocets have pied plumage – more white than black – and graceful proportions with long, bluish legs and a long, very thin, gently upcurved bill.

● Oystercatchers are unmistakable, with their bold black-and-white plumage, pinkish legs and stout, bright orange-red bills. When alarmed, they utter loud, piping calls.

SANDERLING *Calidris alba*

The sanderling is a distinctive small wader, which looks all white at a distance and is generally seen running very quickly in and out of the surf of breaking waves, snapping up tiny items of food. In winter, the upperparts are pale grey with white feather edges and the bird has a dark shoulder mark. In flight, the wings show conspicuous white wingbars. In all plumages the bill, eyes and legs are black. The plumage of juvenile birds resembles that of winter adults, but has a pinkish tinge.

- **SIZE**
  20–21cm (8–8¼in)

- **BREEDING**
  Does not breed in British Isles

- **FOOD**
  Small insects on tundra, tiny marine invertebrates and kelp flies on shore

- **HABITAT**
  Breeds on Arctic tundra; overwinters on sandy shores

- **VOICE**
  Short, hard *'plitt'* alarm call, heard as a louder twittering in chorus from flocks

- **DISTRIBUTION**
  Common winter visitor to British coastline

Sanderlings that linger on British shores until late spring or return by early autumn are occasionally seen in reddish, black-spotted breeding plumage, such as this one.

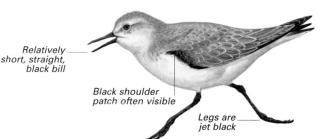

Relatively short, straight, black bill

Black shoulder patch often visible

Legs are jet black

CURLEW SANDPIPER *Calidris ferruginea*

This small but relatively long-legged wader has a longish downcurved bill. Winter adults are pale grey above and pure white below, with fine grey streaking on the upper chest. Most birds seen in Britain are juveniles, with greyish, scaly-looking upperparts and an apricot wash on the breast. All the birds show a white rump in flight and white 'eyebrow'. Adults in breeding plumage, which may turn up in late spring or early autumn, are brick red below and mainly dark chestnut above.

- **SIZE**
  19–22cm (7½–9in)

- **BREEDING**
  Does not breed in British Isles

- **FOOD**
  Insects on tundra, marine invertebrates on shore

- **HABITAT**
  Breeds on Arctic tundra, overwinters on tropical African shores; bays and estuaries en route

- **VOICE**
  A brief, soft, trilling or twittering *'churrip'*

- **DISTRIBUTION**
  Passage migrant; small numbers seen on coasts mainly in spring and autumn

Juvenile curlew sandpipers are more likely to be seen than adults, feeding in the shallows of brackish coastal lagoons.

Rather long, downcurved black bill

Pale breast

Long black legs

DUNLIN *Calidris alpina*

An abundant small coastal wader, the dunlin inhabits most types of shore in winter, but particularly muddy estuaries. A breeding adult has a large black belly patch, but the winter plumage has few striking features, being grey-brown above with a grey-streaked breast and white underparts. However, the dunlin has a noticeably tapered, slightly downcurved black bill and black legs. It forages over wet mud near the water, probing for small animals with a rapid 'stitching' action.

- **SIZE**
  16–20cm (6¼–8in)

- **NEST**
  Hollow, often in a grass tussock, lined with grass or leaves

- **BREEDING**
  Lays 4 pale green eggs spotted with dark brown, in May–June

- **FOOD**
  Molluscs, worms, tiny crustaceans and insects

- **HABITAT**
  Breeds on wet upland moors and salt marshes; winters on coastal mudflats and salt marshes, and on inland marshes

- **VOICE**
  Rough, wheezy *'treep'* flight call; piping, trilling song on breeding grounds

- **DISTRIBUTION**
  Very common on all coasts in winter; uplands in summer

A dumpy-looking bird, the dunlin is the most common wader on British and Irish shores in winter.

Rather plain head

Slightly downcurved black bill

Medium length black legs

K N O T *Calidris canutus*

A medium-sized wader with a shortish, straight bill, the knot has fine white wingbars and a pale grey rump. It congregates in large, and sometimes huge, flocks on the shore in winter, when adults look mostly grey above and white below. Summer adults are striking, being brick-red below and buff above with chestnut and buff patches. Juveniles resemble winter adults, but with scaly upperparts and orange-buff tinged underparts. Knots are always reluctant to move off the shore as the tide advances, but eventually leave in a mass flock to roost on dry ground.

● **SIZE**
23–26cm (9–10½in)

● **BREEDING**
Does not breed in British Isles

● **FOOD**
Insects on tundra, marine invertebrates on seashore

● **HABITAT**
Breeds on Arctic tundra; overwinters on sheltered coasts and large sandy estuaries

● **VOICE**
A short nasal *'knutt'*

● **DISTRIBUTION**
Abundant winter visitor to much of the British coastline

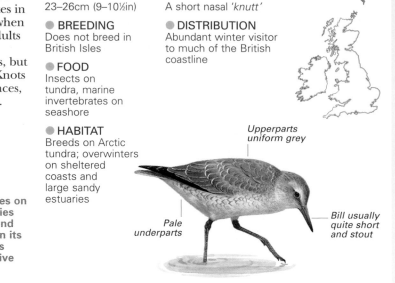

Upperparts uniform grey

Pale underparts

Bill usually quite short and stout

The knot lives on large estuaries in autumn and winter, when its plumage has few distinctive features.

P U R P L E   S A N D P I P E R *Calidris maritima*

This is a plump, short-legged wader with a shortish, very slightly downcurved bill. The upperparts are dark grey in winter with some pale feather edges. The underparts are paler with dark streaks on the breast. The dark bill has a yellowish base in winter, and the legs are mustard yellow or sometimes orange-brown. Spring adults have dark purplish brown, chestnut and whitish marks. Juveniles are similar, but more scaly looking.

● **SIZE**
20–22cm (8–9in)

● **BREEDING**
Does not breed in British Isles

● **FOOD**
Insects, spiders, some plant matter on tundra; marine invertebrates on shore

● **HABITAT**
Breeds on Arctic tundra and moors; overwinters on rocky shores

● **VOICE**
Usually silent, but may give twittering *'quit'* call when taking off

● **DISTRIBUTION**
Common winter visitor, preferring exposed rocky headlines

Plumage mainly grey, with purple sheen seen only in good light

Pale grey below with dark streaks

Mustard yellow or orange-brown legs

Base of black bill yellowish in winter

The purple sandpiper is the darkest of the small waders. It prefers to feed on rocks near the breaking waves.

T U R N S T O N E *Arenaria interpres*

The short-billed turnstone has dark greyish brown upperparts in winter, a dark U-shaped mark below the breast, white underparts, and dull orange legs. Juveniles resemble adults, but their feathers have a more scaly look. A breeding male has clear black-and-white facial markings and chestnut upperparts with dark bands. The female is similar but duller.

● **SIZE**
21–24cm (8¼–9½in)

● **BREEDING**
Does not breed in British Isles

● **FOOD**
Insects on tundra; marine invertebrates on shore

● **HABITAT**
Breeds on Arctic tundra, overwinters on mainly shingly, rocky coasts where seaweed is plentiful

● **VOICE**
Short, metallic *'tuk-a-tuk'* flight calls when feeding birds are disturbed

● **DISTRIBUTION**
Common winter visitor

Breeding male's head is marked with bold black and white

Underparts white

Legs bright orange in summer

Outside the breeding season, the turnstone's comparatively drab, mottled greyish brown and white plumage gives it good camouflage on rocky coasts.

REDSHANK *Tringa totanus*

Slightly smaller and more compact than the spotted redshank, this common wader has a medium-length, straight, black-tipped red bill and fairly long reddish orange legs. All year, adults have greyish brown upperparts, flecked or scalloped with paler markings, but when breeding the breast plumage is heavily spotted, with a chequerboard appearance that is not present in other plumages or on juveniles.

In winter, the redshank moves to estuaries all round the coast whereas in summer it is found on its breeding grounds on coastal marshes and inland wetlands.

● SIZE
27–29cm (10½–11½in)

● NEST
Shallow, lined scrape near tussock

● BREEDING
Lays 4 buffish eggs with reddish brown blotches, mainly in May

● FOOD
Crustaceans, molluscs and marine worms; earthworms and insect larvae inland

● HABITAT
Coasts and estuaries in winter; breeds on coastal salt marshes, freshwater marshes, wet grassland and moorland

● VOICE
Loud, ringing 'teu-heu-heu' alarm call in flight; yodelling, repeated 'tu-yoo, tu-yoo' song

● DISTRIBUTION
Common on coasts in winter, most breed in north and west

Long, straight bill with red base

Spangled grey-brown breeding plumage

Longish red legs, brightest during breeding season

SPOTTED REDSHANK *Tringa erythropus*

A slender wader with long red legs and a long, mostly dark bill, the spotted redshank has very pale grey winter plumage, grading to white on the underside. It is a very active feeder, often chasing prey, frequently into quite deep water, and sometimes even swimming and up-ending like a duck. The juveniles resemble the adults, but are browner above. The striking breeding plumage is sooty black all over with white-speckled feather margins, but is seen in late summer only.

Some spotted redshanks spend the winter in Britain but more are seen in spring and autumn, on migration to and from south-west Europe and Africa.

● SIZE
29–32cm (11½–12¾in)

● BREEDING
Does not breed in British Isles

● FOOD
Insects on tundra in summer, marine invertebrates on coasts in winter

● HABITAT
Breeds on Arctic tundra; overwinters mainly on coasts, especially coastal marshes, sheltered estuaries and brackish lagoons

● VOICE
A shrill 'chew-itt' alarm or flight call, buzzing display call

● DISTRIBUTION
Winter visitor, mainly to coastal areas; passage migrant in spring and autumn

Long, slender bill, red at base

Long legs darkest during summer

Breeding plumage sooty black with white spots

GREENSHANK *Tringa nebularia*

This elegant wader is predominantly greyish above, spangled with black and white, with a long, slightly upturned bill. It is darker in spring and summer, when its back has black patches and more streaks, and there are more dark arrowhead marks on the neck and breast. Juveniles resemble adults, but with buff edges to their darker back feathers, neater streaks along the body and a slightly shorter, straighter bill.

Often wading in deep water, the greenshank walks with long strides and, like the spotted redshank, is an energetic feeder, sometimes running quite fast after prey.

● SIZE
30–34cm (12–13½in)

● NEST
Shallow scrape on ground near rock or grass tussock

● BREEDING
Lays 4 buff eggs with brown markings, in April–May

● FOOD
Aquatic invertebrates, including insects in summer, plus tadpoles and tiny fish

● HABITAT
Bogs and marshes in summer; coastal marshes, estuaries and lakes in winter

● VOICE
Ringing 'chew chew chew'

● DISTRIBUTION
Some breed in Scotland; some overwinter in south and west; autumn passage migrant elsewhere

Long, robust bill has slight upward kink near tip

Colour of long greenish legs most obvious in breeding birds

BAR-TAILED GODWIT *Limosa lapponica*

The bar-tailed godwit's very long bill has a shallow upcurve along its length. It has a barred tail in all plumages, but this is often hard to see. Breeding birds – not often seen in Britain – have a reddish hue, brighter in males than females. Non-breeding birds and juveniles are buffish grey with more chequered dark and pale upperparts. In flight, they lack distinct bars on the upperwings and show white underwings without dark borders. The lower back and rump are white.

In the bar-tailed godwit, far less leg shows above the joint than in the black-tailed godwit.

● **SIZE**
37–39cm (14½–15½in)

● **BREEDING**
Does not breed in British Isles

● **FOOD**
In winter, marine worms, shrimps and other invertebrates; in summer, flies, beetles, worms, some plant matter

● **HABITAT**
Breeds on tundra; overwinters on muddy estuaries

● **VOICE**
Harsh *'kirrick'* flight call; shrill *'krick'* of alarm

● **DISTRIBUTION**
Winter visitor to all major estuaries

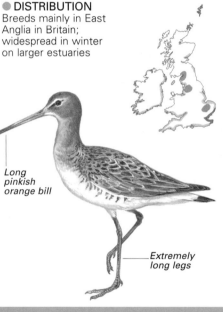

Very long bill with upward tilt

Breeding male has dark, rusty red underside and mottled brown upperparts

BLACK-TAILED GODWIT *Limosa limosa*

Compared to the slightly smaller bar-tailed godwit, this species has longer legs and a black terminal band on the tail, and a straight bill. Breeding birds are reddish brown on head and neck, but non-breeding, winter birds are greyish brown with paler underparts. In flight, the black-and-white pattern on the wings is conspicuous. The white underwings have dark borders.

The longer legs of the black-tailed godwit help distinguish the two godwit species, as do its white wingbars and black-banded tail.

● **SIZE**
40–44cm (16–17½in)

● **NEST**
Shallow scrape in grassy terrain

● **BREEDING**
Lays 3–4 dark-spotted olive to brown eggs in April–May

● **FOOD**
Worms, molluscs and other invertebrates

● **HABITAT**
Breeds in damp meadows; overwinters on estuaries and coastal marshes

● **VOICE**
Chattering calls; nasal *'kee-vit'* and loud *'weeka-weeka-weeka'* at breeding sites

● **DISTRIBUTION**
Breeds mainly in East Anglia in Britain; widespread in winter on larger estuaries

Long pinkish orange bill

Extremely long legs

CURLEW *Numenius arquata*

This is a large, long-legged wader with an extremely long, downcurved bill. Its plumage is mostly brown above, with dark brown streaks on the neck and breast, arrow-shaped marks on the flanks and bars on the back, grading to white below the tail. Females are generally larger, with longer bills. In winter, the lower mandible is flesh coloured. The beautiful bubbling song of the curlew is heard frequently on upland breeding grounds.

The curlew is the largest European wader, with the longest bill. It breeds on moorland, but is common on coasts in winter.

● **SIZE**
50–57cm (20–22½in)

● **NEST**
Large scrape near tussock, with grassy lining

● **BREEDING**
Lays 2–5 green or olive eggs with darker spots and blotches in April–June

● **FOOD**
Marine worms, molluscs and crabs on coast, other invertebrates inland

● **HABITAT**
Breeds mainly in uplands; overwinters on coasts, estuaries and marshes

● **VOICE**
Sad *'cour-leee'* call; song is a bubbling trill given in display flight

● **DISTRIBUTION**
Widespread breeding bird in north and west, overwinters on coasts

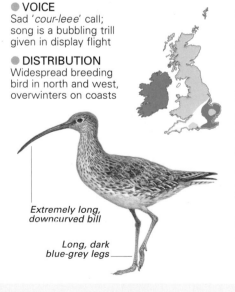

Extremely long, downcurved bill

Long, dark blue-grey legs

WHIMBREL *Numenius phaeopus*

Smaller than the curlew, but similar in appearance, the whimbrel has dark stripes on its head and a pale 'eyebrow' that show well at close range. Its plumage often looks darker than the curlew's. The whimbrel's bill is shorter and curves more abruptly nearer the tip, and in flight the bird looks smaller and has faster wingbeats. Its calls are different, although it uses a snatch of curlew-like song in display. Juveniles resemble adults, but have buff spots on the crown and wing coverts. It is usually seen in small groups.

Almost all of the 500 or so whimbrels that breed in Britain do so on Shetland. Outside the breeding season, whimbrels occur as passage migrants around the coast.

● SIZE
40–42cm (16–16½in)

● NEST
Shallow scrape, lined with plant material

● BREEDING
Lays 3–4 olive to buff, dark-spotted eggs from mid-April to May

● FOOD
Insects, marine worms and small crustaceans

● HABITAT
Breeds mainly on Arctic tundra and uplands; winters on seashores

● VOICE
Main call is an often seven-note rippling trill; short curlew-like song with terminal trill

● DISTRIBUTION
Scarce breeding bird in Scotland, passage migrant on coasts elsewhere

Distinctive dark and pale stripes on head

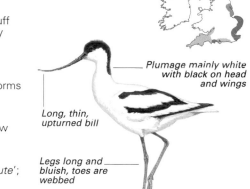

Chest darker than curlew's

AVOCET *Recurvirostra avosetta*

The avocet has a long, slender upturned bill and very long blue-grey legs. It looks brilliant white from a distance, but closer views show a black crown, nape and black wing panels. Juveniles have dark brown smudgy markings in place of black. These large waders are often seen feeding in flocks on mudflats, sweeping through mud with their bills.

Avocets breed on shallow coastal pools. In winter, large numbers congregate on estuaries, mainly in the south-west, notably on the estuaries of the River Exe and River Tamar.

● SIZE
42–45cm (16½–18in)

● NEST
Shallow scrape near water, lined with aquatic plants

● BREEDING
Lays 3–4 blotchy buff eggs, mainly in May

● FOOD
Mainly small mud-dwelling insects, crustaceans and worms

● HABITAT
Estuaries, coastal marshes and shallow lagoons

● VOICE
Melodious '*klute klute*'; harsher calls when alarmed

● DISTRIBUTION
Breeds on east and south coast of England, overwinters mainly on estuaries in south-west

Plumage mainly white with black on head and wings

Long, thin, upturned bill

Legs long and bluish, toes are webbed

OYSTERCATCHER *Haematopus ostralegus*

This striking black-and-white wader has a long orange bill, red eyes and coral pink legs. In winter, adults acquire a white chin stripe on the black neck. Newly hatched chicks and juveniles have remarkable camouflage, which blends perfectly with lichen-covered rocks. In their first winter, young birds are paler than adults, with a larger white throat patch. Birds in large flocks are excitable, frequently giving shrill, piping calls.

Oystercatchers nest on rocky shores around the British coast, especially in the north and west. They congregate on estuaries in winter, forming spectacular high-tide roosts.

● SIZE
40–45cm (16–18in)

● NEST
Shallow gravel-lined scrape on open ground

● BREEDING
Lays 3 blotchy buff eggs in April–May

● FOOD
Mainly bivalve molluscs on coasts, earthworms when inland

● HABITAT
Rocky shores, estuaries, increasingly along rivers, especially with shingle banks for nesting; also shores of lakes, flooded gravel pits and reservoirs

● VOICE
Far-carrying piping calls such as '*kleep, kleep*'; loud '*ku-beek*' of alarm

● DISTRIBUTION
Common breeding bird on coasts; also inland, mainly in north

Stout body with pied plumage

Heavy, robust orange-red bill

Pink legs

Barnacles

Cemented to the rocks of exposed tidal shores, and protected by strong plates of stony armour, barnacles are able to survive conditions that would kill most other creatures. As a result, they have few competitors, and flourish in their billions.

Life is tough for the wildlife of rocky tidal shores. Hours of exposure at low tide, when the rocks are dried out by wind and sun – or drenched in fresh water by rain – are interspersed with periods of turmoil when waves crash on to the shore with shattering force. Only a few types of animals are able to tolerate the harsh conditions, and of these, the barnacles are perhaps the most successful.

A barnacle's winning formula involves sheltering within an armoured housing that is cemented to the rock, and sealing itself inside whenever conditions become too extreme. The armour consists of a volcano-shaped ring of chalky plates, with an opening at the top that can be closed by a pair of sliding doors. The barnacle lies inside on its back, with its six pairs of legs projecting upward through the opening and raking the water for food.

Despite appearances, barnacles are crustaceans – relatives of shrimps and crabs – but their way of life requires a drastic modification of the normal crustacean body, transforming it into something that looks more like a limpet, which is a mollusc. Early naturalists were misled by this, and the true affinities of barnacles became clear only when an amateur naturalist netted some barnacle larvae – which do look like crustaceans – and watched them transform into adults.

Planktonic larvae

A barnacle's life history is remarkable. Each adult bears organs of both sexes, but to breed successfully they must exchange sperm with their neighbours on the rock surface to fertilise each other's eggs. To achieve this, each barnacle grows an enormous male organ in late summer or autumn. Relative to the animal's overall body size, it is probably the longest penis in the animal kingdom, about ten times the height of its shell. The barnacle stretches it across to penetrate the shell of a neighbour of the same species. In mixed populations, each individual has to probe around until it finds another barnacle of its own kind.

The fertilised eggs are stored within the barnacle's armoured body throughout the winter. Each egg then becomes a tiny mobile larva called a 'nauplius'. Released into the sea in spring, the larvae live in the plankton for a few weeks, moulting about six times as they grow. The last moult results in a second-stage larva called a 'cyprid', after another species of tiny crustacean that it strongly resembles.

▼ **Barnacles such as** *Balanus perforatus* **start to feed when they are covered by the rising tide. The shell plates move apart, allowing six pairs of hair-fringed limbs to emerge and sift the water for potential food.**

▶ **The most common barnacle of rocky shores is the acorn barnacle,** *Semibalanus balanoides.* **The low, greyish white cones form dense clusters that can completely cover the rock of the 'barnacle zone'.**

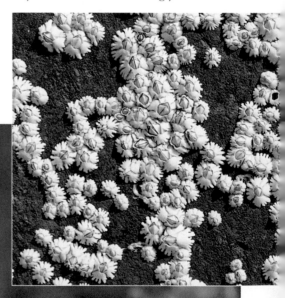

▲ Every year, each barnacle grows a thin penis, with which it fertilises the eggs of a neighbour. Its extreme length is necessary because the animals are fixed to the rock, and cannot move any closer together.

The cyprid does not feed, because its only purpose is to select a suitable site on which to change into a juvenile barnacle. The larvae must settle close to each other, so they are attracted only to hard surfaces that carry a barnacle scent. These will either have living barnacles already on them, or bear the remains of dead ones.

Once settled, the barnacle attaches itself to the rock and grows its protective armour plates. The cement with which the animals attach themselves is strong enough to resist anything the sea can throw at them, and even a direct hit by a wave-tossed rock will usually result in just the top layer of plates being knocked off, leaving the base of the animal still attached to the surface. Indeed, the barnacle's 'glue' is so effective that it has provided chemists with a model for developing extra-strong synthetic industrial adhesives.

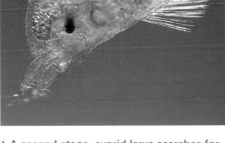

▲ A second-stage, cyprid larva searches for a hard surface where it can prepare for metamorphosis into a hard-shelled adult. Once it has settled it will never move again.

Barnacle zone

There are about 20 species of barnacle in British waters, but two species are much commoner than the others. *Chthamalus stellatus* is found high on the shore, while *Semibalanus balanoides* occurs slightly lower down. They form a grey band at the high-water mark on cliffs and boulders, and give their name to the 'barnacle zone' of the seashore. Both species have six shell-plates, but *C. stellatus* has a kite-shaped top opening, while that of *S. balanoides* is

▲ These milky coloured barnacles are newly settled and recently transformed from the second larval stage. They will become fully mature in about a year.

diamond-shaped. *Balanus perforatus* is shaped like a volcano while another common barnacle, the wart barnacle – with the apt scientific name *Verruca stroemia* – has a more ragged shell, composed of just four asymmetrical ribbed plates. A smoother four-plated species is *Elminius modestus*, a native of Australasia which probably arrived on the bottoms of ships.

Very different are the stalked barnacles occasionally found on stranded driftwood. The most common of these are goose barnacles, *Lepas anatifera*, which have bluish grey body plates on brown stalks. They feed just like other barnacles, but are not adapted to resist tidal exposure or the pounding of the waves.

PARASITIC BARNACLES

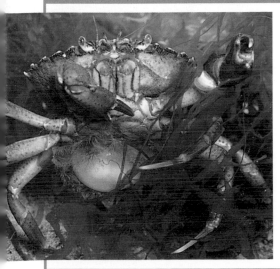

Some species of barnacles are parasites that feed on other living animals. The cyprid larvae settle on potential hosts and bore into their bodies. They grow a mass of 'roots' that absorb nutrients from the animals' body fluids. In the case of *Sacculina carcini*, the host is usually a common shore crab. The cyprid larva enters the crab's gill chamber and penetrates its tissues. In time, the barnacle develops an external pouch of eggs, which can often be seen projecting from the crab's abdomen. Eventually, the next generation will be released into the sea to seek new hosts.

The egg sac beneath the body of this shore crab shows that it has been infected by *Sacculina carcini*. Although not necessarily fatal, this often results in degeneration of the crab's reproductive tissues, so it cannot breed.

WILDLIFE WATCH

Where can I see barnacles?

● Barnacles cover large areas of rock on the middle shore, forming a pale band above the blue-black mussel zone and below a zone of black lichens.

● Find a rock pool at mid-shore level on a falling tide. Lie full length and look for submerged barnacles. Watch closely to see the delicate limbs extend from the holes in the tops of the shells and rake the water for food.

The lugworm

Unlike most animals, the lugworm breeds in winter. Mass spawning involves every lugworm on a beach for several days, and is part of a strict timetable that dominates every hour of this creature's burrowing life.

Most animals that live on sandy beaches spend much of their time buried invisibly in the sand. They may emerge to feed at high tide, when they are covered by water, but when the tide ebbs away they disappear. The exceptions to this are the lugworms, which live in their millions on sandy and muddy tidal beaches. These animals burrow into the sand and never voluntarily emerge from their burrows, even at high water, but their presence is given away by their casts – ragged knots of sand ejected at the surface. Even in the depths of winter, many beaches exposed at low tide are covered by these lugworm casts, showing that the animals are busy feeding below.

Swallowing sand

Lugworms are segmented, annelid worms related to earthworms, with retractable bristles, or chaetae, on their bodies that help them burrow through wet sand. Six species live on British coasts, the most widespread being the blow lug or lobworm. They all feed in the same way, by swallowing sand to extract any organic nutrients that may be mixed with it.

To burrow, the lugworm pushes its knobbly pharynx or proboscis from its mouth and dabbles it into the surface of wet sand to liquefy it. The lugworm sinks headfirst into the wet cavity it has made, and gains a purchase on the sand by expanding its cylindrical body. It pulls down the rear part of its body, pushes out its proboscis again and repeats the cycle.

As the lugworm tunnels into the sand, it smears the burrow walls with mucus to keep them intact, forming a vertical tube. When the burrow reaches about 50cm (20in) deep, the animal turns to make a horizontal gallery. About 10cm (4in) farther on it tunnels a short way towards the surface, creating a J-shaped burrow.

Lying in the deepest part of its tunnel, the lugworm is now ready to feed. Using waves of contraction passing from front to rear of its body, it pumps water and sand towards its mouth. It ingests the sand and draws it into its gut to absorb any organic matter that it contains. Ingesting sand from in front of its mouth makes more sand drop from the surface towards its head. This creates a vertical hole, making the worm's burrow a perfect U-shape and opening a shallow crater at the surface.

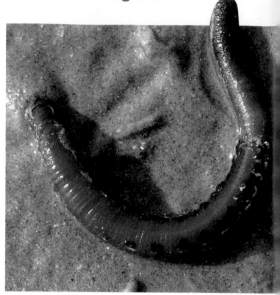

▲ If it is exposed on the surface, a lugworm is vulnerable to the many hungry birds that feed on beaches, especially in winter, so it rapidly plunges its head into the sand and burrows out of sight.

▼ At low tide, most sandy shores are studded with lugworm casts. The more organic material there is in the sand, the more lugworms there will be, and muddy beaches can support huge populations.

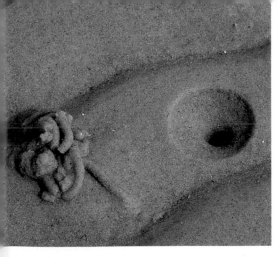

The head shaft of a lugworm's burrow is marked by a shallow depression, often with a hole in the middle, which lies 10–15cm (4–6in) from the familiar coils of voided sand that mark the tail shaft.

The lugworm's feeding bouts are not randomly based on hunger, but recur punctually every seven minutes. After every five or six of these feeding cycles the lugworm reverses up its burrow to void a gutful of sand at the surface. This can be a dangerous business because it brings the worm within range of long-billed shorebirds, such as the curlew. At the first sign of attack – which could be as subtle as a vibration of the sand as a bird approaches – an alarm reflex sends a nerve impulse from the lugworm's tail towards its head through a set of special nerve pathways. These impulses travel 60 times faster than those passing down the standard nerves, and make the worm dig in the bristles at its front end and contract its tail. Even if it is not quick enough, all is not lost – its gills and other essential organs are near its head, so they remain intact if the worm loses its rear end.

Winter spawning

As it feeds, a lugworm must have a fresh supply of oxygenated water. It maintains this by a third cycle that is interspersed with the feeding and excretion cycles. Waves of contraction pump water across 13 pairs of gills near the lugworm's front end, and irrigate the burrow to prevent it

LUGWORM FACT FILE

Lugworms are the most common marine worms of sandy shores. Their casts are a familiar sight on most beaches, from the middle shore downwards, indicating where they have dug their U-shaped burrows in the sand.

● **NAMES**
Common names: lugworm, lobworm, blow lug, yellowtail
Scientific name: *Arenicola marina*

● **HABITAT**
Sandy and muddy beaches

● **DISTRIBUTION**
All around British and Irish coasts

● **STATUS**
Very common

● **SIZE**
Length 15–25cm (6–10in); diameter 15–20mm (⅝–¾in)

● **KEY FEATURES**
Dark sandy brown, tinged with red or deep pink; body segmented, thicker at front; short bristles project from every segment; 13 pairs of gills; pharynx is pushed through mouth to form trumpet-shaped proboscis

● **FOOD**
Organic detritus from among sand grains

● **BREEDING**
Breeds mainly in November or December; sperm is drawn into female's burrow where eggs are fertilised

● **YOUNG**
Larvae develop first in sand, later on surface in mucous tubes, then in plankton while still in mucous tubes; finally settle on suitable sand or mud to start burrowing

Distribution map key

▨ Present

☐ Not present

The body becomes narrower towards the tail.

Gills are red and feathery.

Fewer bristles grow on the front part of body.

Tail is thin and smooth.

from becoming foul. This is particularly important if the lugworm has burrowed into the smelly, black layer of sand that lies 20–30cm (8–12in) below the surface. Here there is very little oxygen but high levels of toxic hydrogen sulphide, which would poison the lugworm if it did not have a clean water supply.

In late autumn and winter, a beach's entire lugworm population spawns in the sea within a few days. The water carries the male's sperm into burrows of the females, where it fertilises their eggs.

These develop into larvae that leave the burrow and are carried to just below the low-water mark. Here they settle among the coarser sediments for a few months in temporary mucous tubes. When they are about 10mm (⅜in) long they migrate up the shore, while still in their mucous tubes, to settle in the organically rich zone just below the strand line. Over time they gradually move down the beach to colonise the wet, muddy sand of the lower shore, where they may live as adults for another six years.

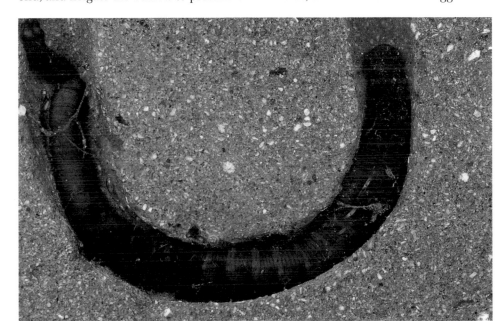

WILDLIFE WATCH

Where can I see lugworms?

● Lugworm casts can be found on almost any sheltered sandy or muddy beach at low tide. By watching the sand carefully, the worms can be seen extruding their casts on to the surface.

● With patience, it is possible to time the lugworm's casting cycle, which usually takes precisely 40 minutes.

With each high tide the current sweeps fresh sand into the head shaft of the lugworm's U-shaped burrow, allowing it to live in the same place for weeks at a time without running out of food.

Sea mats

The minute creatures that form encrusting sea mats are so small that they are hardly recognisable with the naked eye. A close look under a lens reveals whole colonies of delicate, specialised organisms with a fragile beauty of their own.

The kelp that is swept up on beaches by winter storms is often encrusted with curious sheets that resemble woven textiles. Although these look almost artificial, they are actually animals called sea mats. Each sheet is a colony made up of many individuals, or 'zooids', that live in partnership, rather like the individual polyps of a colonial coral. Each zooid is housed in its own box-like compartment, and each has its own function in the colony. Many are feeding zooids that extend waving tentacles to snare plankton, but others are equipped with tiny paddles that help circulate water around the sea mat, bringing food and removing waste. Some are specialised for defence, with minute 'beaks' that they use to deter or remove small organisms that might interfere with the functioning of the whole colony. These specialists are linked to the rest of the colony by pores that allow the exchange of nutrients, so they do not need to spend time gathering their own food.

Sea mats are very numerous animals, particularly in shallow, temperate seas. Some relatives occur in fresh water. They have a wide variety of body forms, ranging from flat sheets to hard lumps and delicate, plant-like tufts, but they all function in much the same way.

Spreading colonies

The sea mat that forms colonies on kelp is usually *Membranipora membranacea*. It can cover large areas, with millions of individual compartments or boxes, each neatly anchored to its neighbour, forming a veneer-like layer over the host's fronds. The colony has a leading edge where growth is vigorous, with a high density of active zooids. Seen underwater, this part of the colony has a furry look, rather like moss. Behind this, in the older part of the

ZOOID COLONY

Each zooid of a sea mat colony lives in its own tiny, rectangular compartment, from which it can extend itself by fluid pressure generated by the contraction of its muscles. When extended, each of the feeding zooids filters plankton from the surrounding water with the whorl of tentacles around its mouth, retreating quickly if danger threatens. Sea slugs and sea spiders feed well on sea mats whenever they have the chance.

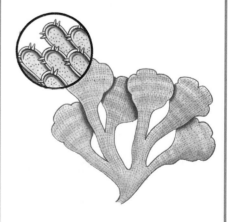

Some sea mats, such as hornwrack, grow in free-standing colonies, forming bushy clumps with flexible, flat branches that fork regularly. Minute compartments cover both sides.

The sea mat *Bugula flabellata* grows in tufted, branching colonies on rocks on the lower shore. It favours shaded overhangs and is often found alongside sponges, red seaweeds and other organisms.

Tangled swathes of seaweed fronds and stems provide safe anchorages for several species, notably the hairy sea mat, *Electra pilosa*, seen here forming an irregular branched mass among an egg wrack's brown, bean-shaped air bladders.

colony, there may be a lot of empty compartments where the older zooids have died off and fallen away.

The mossy appearance of living sea mat colonies misled early naturalists into believing that they were plants, and they were not recognised as animals until the middle of the 18th century, when they became known as the Bryozoa, meaning 'moss animals'. In the 1950s zoologists started calling them Ectoprocta but they are still more generally known as Bryozoa, or bryozoans.

Drifting larvae

Different species of sea mats prefer to colonise different kinds of surface. *Membranipora membranacea* settles on rocks as well as on kelp and other algae. A hairy species called *Flustrellidra hispida* is common on the stems and holdfasts (the tough, adhesive stem end) of wrack, and a bright orange and solid form, *Umbonula littoralis*, usually settles on rock. Some bryozoans, such as *Flustra foliacea* or hornwrack, and the misleadingly named ross or rose coral, *Pentapora foliacea*, form self-supporting, leaf-like colonies.

Each sea mat colony usually contains males and females, although individual zooids can be hermaphrodite, with both male and female sex organs. Despite this, they do not fertilise themselves, but exchange sperm with other colonies.

Most species retain their fertilised eggs in a brood pouch until they hatch. The larvae then emerge to seek settlement sites. They drift with the plankton, and many fail to find sites that suit their often precise needs. Sea mats that colonise seaweeds, for example, may settle only on certain parts of the host, such as the base of the stem or the holdfast.

The first zooid to form from a settled larva is called the ancestrula, and from this single individual a colony soon develops by budding – a kind of cloning. As the colony grows, it keeps pace with the growth of a living host. Those that settle on annual seaweeds, which lose their fronds at the end of the season, usually expand downwards towards the holdfast. This ensures that when the frond breaks off, a healthy part of the sea mat colony is left behind. This will expand into a bigger colony the following year, when the new frond grows.

Around 5000 species of sea mats exist worldwide, and several hundred live in European waters. Some may become a nuisance, such as the species that settle on ships' hulls and have to be cleaned off to maintain the efficiency of the hull and save fuel. Other species settle in the cooling pipes of power stations, where they can reduce the pipe's bore by more than half. However, most sea mats are harmless, intriguing organisms, and when seen under a microscope or lens they can even be described as beautiful.

WILDLIFE WATCH

Where can I see sea mats?

● Many species of sea mat occur all around the coasts of Britain, but the greatest variety is to be found in the warmer waters of the south and west.

● Rock overhangs provide a combination of anchorage and shade for many sea mats. When searching in awkward places, take care to avoid being cut off by tides.

● Other sea mats favour holdfasts and fronds of larger seaweeds, so search at extreme low water or study seaweeds beached by the tide.

● It is essential to use a hand lens when examining sea mats in order to reveal their complex structure.

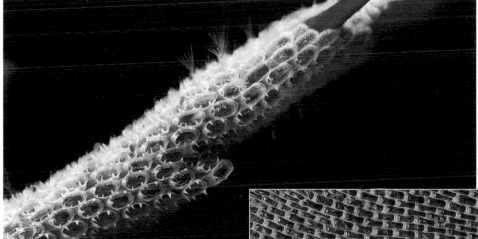

▲ Fine tentacled zooids, just visible to the naked eye, emerge from each compartment of this hairy sea mat to trap food particles. This species forms an irregular white crust on seaweeds and rocks.

▶ Colonies of *Membranipora membranacea* regularly encrust fronds of kelp and resemble fine white lace. They consist of delicate, rectangular compartments, as seen here enlarged, with a blunt spine at each corner.

Index

Photographs: Front cover: Main image: Nigel Hicks/Woodfall Wild Images; Inset: Roger Tidman/FLPA (oystercatcher); Back cover: NHPA/B.Loster; 1 FLPA/Flip De Nooyer/Foto Natura; 2-3 Ashley Cooper/Woodfall Wild Images (Derwent Water & Keswick); 4 NV; 5 (t) FLPA/J.Watkins, (b)Tom Walmsley; 6 (bl,bc,br) NP/Paul Sterry; 7(bl) NP, (bc,br) NP/Paul Sterry; 8(c) NP/P.Boag, (bl) NP/Andrew Cleave, (br) NP/Paul Sterry; 9(bl, bc) NP/Paul Sterry, (br) NP; 10-11 Rebecca Fong/ Alamy (river walk); 12(cl) FLPA/H.Hautala, (sp) FLPA/J.Watkins, 13(tl) GPL/Anne Green-Armytage, (tr)Garden Matters, (bc) NP/N.Phelps, (br) NP/Paul Sterry; 14(tr) BC/B.Glover, (bl) Ardea/Chris Knights; 15(tl) BC/J.McDonald, (b) NP/R.Bush; 16(b) Ardea/B.Gibbons; 17(tr) Ardea/J.Daniels, (bc) Ardea/Dennis Avon, (br) Ardea/B.Gibbons; 18(tl) FLPA/Richard Brooks, (tr) NHPA/Gerry Cambridge, English Nature/Pete Wakely; 19(tl) FLPA/Leo Vogelzang, (tr) FLPA/Foto Natura, (cr) FLPA/Roger Tidman; 20(tl) Ardea/I.Beames, (cr) FLPA/Nigel Catlinn, (bc) NSc; 21(br) Ardea/John Daniels; 22(bl) OSF, (bc) NP, (br) NP; 23(tr) NP, (c) NV/David Harrison; 24(cl) NP/A.Cleave, (bl) NP/D.Osbourne, (b) NP; 25(tru,tr) NP, (cr) NP/SC.Bisserot; 26(tr) NP/Paul Sterry, (cr) NP/R.Tidman, (bl) NP/B.Burtidge, (br) NP/D.Osbourne; 27(bl,br) NP; 28(tr) NV/Heather Angel, (b) FLPA; 29(cl) NP/Michael J Hammet, (cr) BC/Michael Glover; 30(cu) BC/Jeff Foot Productions, (cr) FLPA/ DP.Wilson, (bcu) FLPA/ DP.Wilson, (bl) FLPA/DP.Wilson, (b) NP/Paul Sterry; 31(clu,cl,bl) NV; 32(tl) BC, (tr) FLPA/Tony Hamblin, (br) BC; 33(tl) NP/Paul Sterry, (tr) FLPA/A.R.Hamblin, (b) NP/EA Janes; 34(tru, tr) NP/Paul Sterry, (cl) NPL/A.Cooper, (b) NPL/PN.Johnson; 35(tl) NP/A.Cleave, (tr) NPL/N.Benvie, (cl) FLPA/DP.Wilson, (br) NP/A.Cleave; 36(tr,cl,br) NP, (bl) NHPA/Hellio & Van Ingen; 37(tl) NHPA/D.Woodfall, (tr) NPL/Rob Tilley, (b) FLPA/MJ.Thomas; 38(b) Cumbria Wildlife Trust/J.Ketchen; 39(tr)BC/Hans Reinhard, (cr) FLPA/Roger Wilmhurst, (br) BC/Gordon Langsbury; 40(tl) BC/Michael McKavett, (bl) BC/WS.Paton, (b) Cumbria Wildlife Trust/J.Ketchen; 41(tr) BC/Konrad Wohte, (br) BC; 42(tl) NV, (tr)BC/Felix Lathardt, (c,bru) BC/Wayne Lenkinen, (bl) NV; 44-45 Wim Klomp/Foto Natura/FLPA (Bittern); 46(b) NPL/J.Foott; 47(tr) Ardea/Borkowski, BC/Hans Reinhard; 48(tc) BC, (tr) NHPA, (cl) FLPA, (bl) BC/J.Cancolosi, (br) BC/J.Jurka; 49(tl) NPL/J.Foott, (tr) Ardea/S.Meyers, (br) Dembinsky Photo Association/D.Braud; 50(b) NP/EA.Janes; 51(tr) NP/EA.Janes, (b) Planet Earth/P.Kenny; 52(tl) FLPA/R.Lawrence, (tr) NP/P.Knight, (bl) NP/EA.Janes; 53(tl) FLPA/M.Clark, (tr) FLPA/M.Clark, (b) NP/EA.Janes; 54(b) FLPA/Wim Klomp; 55(tr) OSF/T.Bomford, (b) Aquila/C.Graves; 56(cr)FLPA/Jurgen & Christine Sohns, (br) FLPA/D.Ellinger; 57(cl) FLPA/Flip de Nooyer, (c) OSF/D.Green, (cr) NHPA/D.Karp, (bl) NHPA/Hellio & Van Ingen, (bc) Aquila/C.Greaves, (br) FLPA/T.Schenk; 58(bl) FLPA/Silvestris, (bc) FLPA/Y Eshtol; 59(tr) FLPA/W.Klomp, (b) FLPA/D.Hosking; 60(b) Mike Read; 61(cl) NP/D.Osbourne, (br) NP/Paul Sterry; 62(br) Laurie Campbell; 63(tl) Laurie Campbell, (cl) NP/Paul Sterry, (bl) Mike Read; 64(tl,cl,bl) NP/Paul Sterry; 65(tl) NP/Paul Sterry, (cl) NP/WS.Paton, (bl) NP/D.Osbourne, 66(tl,cl,bl) NP/Paul Sterry; 67(bl) Ardea/Geoff Trinder, (br) NPL/Richard du Toit; 68(tr) FLPA/Mike Jones, (b) FLPA/Oene Moedt/Foto Natura; 69(tr) FLPA/ Oene Moedt/Foto Natura, (c) FLPA/Henk Wester/Foto Natura, (cr) OSF/David Tipling, (bl) FLPA/David Hosking, (bc) FLPA/Flip de Nooyer/Foto Natura, (br) NHPA/Jordi Bas Cesas; 70(cr) FLPA/David Hosking, (bl) Ardea/Dennis Avon; 71(t) BC/Kim Taylor; 72(tr) OSF/BP.Kent, (cr) OSF/S.Dalton, (b) BC/Andy Purcell; 73(tl) OSF/BP.Kent, (tr) BC, (bl) FLPA/Rohdich; 74(tl) BC/Kim Taylor, (b) NHPA; 75(t) BC/Hans Reinhard; 76(tr) Nick Giles, (cr) NHPA, (b) Ardea/P.Morris; 77(tl) NHPA/ Hellio Van Ingen, (tr) NHPA, (br) FLPA/A.Maywald; 78(tr) Nick Giles, (b) NV/H.Angel; 79(t) NV, (br) NP; 80(tr) NV, (bl,bc,br) FLPA, 81(t) NP, (br) Nick Giles; 82(tr) NV/Heather Angel, (bcu) NP/SC.Bisserot, (bl) OSF/F.Ehrenstrom; 83 Nick Gordon/ardea.com; 84(br) Laurie Campbell; 85(tr) NP/H.Miles, (bl) NP/H.Miles; 86(tl) WW/Bob Gibbons, (tr) WW/S.Austin, (bl) Laurie Campbell, (bru) NP/H.Miles; 87(tl) NP/H.Miles, (tr) Laurie Campbell, (bl) NP/H.Miles; 88(l) NPL/J.Downer, (br) OSF/M.Binchead; 89(tr) FLPA/BB.Casals, (b) OSF/ R.Redfern; 90(tl) NHPA/EA.Janes; 91(tr) NHPA/Stephen Dalton, (bl) OSF/J.Downer, (br) OSF; 92(bl) NPL/A.Jain; 93(tl) FLPA/FW.Lane, (c) OSF/M.Learch, (b) NV/G.Kinns; 94(t) Tom Walmsley, (b) BC/C&S Hood; 96(tl,bl) Tom Walmsley; 97(tl) Tom Walmsley, (tr) BC/J Foott; 98(tl) OSF/M.Leach, (tr) WW/M.Scott, (bl) Tom Walmsley; 99(tr,b) Tom Walmsley; 100(t) NPL/D.Nill; 101(tr) OSF/P.Kay, (bl) David Chapman; 102(tl) NP/MV/B.Loster, (tr) FLPA/T.Hamblin; 103(tl) David Chapman, (cl) NHPA/J.Lemoigne, (tr) Aquila/M.Bates, (cl) BC/C.Lockwood, (c) Woodfall/ M.Lane, (cr) NV/Heather Angel; 104(tl) BC/A.Potts, (tr) BC/B.Osbourne, (cru) OSF, (bl) WW/M.Lane; 105(tl) BC/Kim Taylor, (tr) David Chapman, (bl) NPL/T.Vezo; 106(c) FLPA/Flip De Nooyer/Foto Natura; 107(tr,b) Andy Rouse; 108(blu) NSc/A.Watts, (bcu) NP/P.Evans, (bru) Aquila, (bl) OSF/R.Packwood, (bc) NV, (br) FLPA/E&D Hosking; 109(tr) David Chapman, (bl) OSF/T.Bomford; 110(bl) OSF/E.Woods, (bc) Aquila/MC.Wilkes, (br) Aquila/MC.Wilkes; 111(tl) FLPA/P.Perry, (tr) FLPA/W.Wismewski; 112(c) OSF/M.Hamblin; 113(tr) BC; 115(tl) Windrush/A.Morris, (cl) Ardea/C.Knight, (bl) FLPA/Oene Moedt/Foto Natura; 116(tl) FLPA/AR.Hamblin, (cl) NHPA/L.Campbell, (bl) FLPA/Roger Tidman; 117(tl) FLPA/T.Hamblin, (cl) FLPA/MB.Withers, (cl) FLPA/T.Hamblin; 118(tl) NP/R.Mearns, (cl) FLPA/W.Wisniewski, (bl) FLPA/MB.Withers; 119(tl) NP/Paul Sterry, (cl) NHPA/Nigel J Dennis, (bl) Ardea/Chris Knights; 120(cr) Ardea, (b) OSF/GI.Barnard; 121(tl) NV/Heather Angel, (tr) OSF/P.Kay, (c) OSF/P.Parks, (bl) OSF/GI.Barnard; 122(tl) NV/Heather Angel, (b) S.Scott; 123(tl) BC/N.Schwirtz, (bl)OSF/London Scientific Films; 124(bl) NV/Heather Angel; 125(tr) NV/Heather Angel, (blu) NV/Heather Angel, (br) NHPA/GI.Barnard.

Illustrations: 19(b) John Ridyard; 29(cr) Midsummer; 43(c) Midsummer; 56-58(t) John Ridyard; 62(t) Robert Morton; 63(r) Robert Morton; 64(r) Robert Morton; 65(r) Robert Morton; 66(r) Robert Morton; 70(t) Brin Edwards/The Art Agency; 90(b) John Ridyard; 92(t) Guy Troughton; 96(tr) Milne Cameron; 97(b) Milne Cameron; 102-103(b) John Ridyard; 108(t) John Ridyard; 109(br) John Ridyard; 110(tl) John Ridyard; 114(t) Brin Edwards/The Art Agency; 115(tr) Richard Lewington, (cr) Tim Hayward, (br) Brin Edwards/The Art Agency; 116(tr,cr) Richard Lewington, (br) Tim Hayward; 117(r) Tim Hayward; 118(r) Tim Hayward; 119(r) Tim Hayward; 123(c) Midsummer.

Key to Photo Library Abbreviations: BC = Bruce Coleman Ltd, FLPA = Frank Lane Photo Agency, GPL = Garden Picture Library, NHPA = Natural History Photo Agency, NI = Natural Image, NP = Nature Photographers, NPL = Nature Picture Library, NSc = Natural Science Photos, NV = Heather Angel/Natural Visions, OSF = Oxford Scientific Films, PW = Premaphotos Wildlife, WW = Woodfall Wild.

Key to position abbreviations: b = bottom, bl = bottom left, blu = bottom left upper, br = bottom right, bru =bottom right upper, c = centre, cl = centre left, clu = centre left upper, cr = centre right, cru = centre right upper, cu = centre upper, l = left, r = right, sp = spread, t = top, tl = top left, tlu = top left upper, tr = top right, tru = top right upper.

Wildlife Watch
Waterside & Coast in Winter

Published by the Reader's Digest Association Limited, 2006

The Reader's Digest Association Limited
11 Westferry Circus, Canary Wharf
London E14 4HE

We are committed to both the quality of our products and the service we provide to our customers, so please feel free to contact us on 08705 113366, or via our website at: www.readersdigest.co.uk

If you have any comments about the content of our books you can contact us at: gbeditorial@readersdigest.co.uk

® Reader's Digest, The Digest and the Pegasus logo are registered trademarks of The Reader's Digest Association, Inc., of Pleasantville, New York, USA

Reader's Digest General Books:
Editorial Director Julian Browne
Art Director Nick Clark
Series Editor Christine Noble
Project Editor Lisa Thomas
Project Art Editor Julie Bennett
Prepress Accounts Manager Penelope Grose

This book was designed, edited and produced by Eaglemoss Publications Ltd, based on material first published as the partwork *Wildlife of Britain*

For Eaglemoss:
Project Editor Marion Paull
Editors Samantha Gray, John Woodward
Art Editor Phil Gibbs
Editorial Assistant Helen Hawksfield
Consultant Jonathan Elphick

Publishing Manager Nina Hathway

Printed and bound in Europe by Arvato Iberia

CONCEPT CODE: UK 0133/G/S
BOOK CODE: 630-013
ISBN: 0 276 44061 7
ORACLE CODE: 356200015H.00.24